What F
Anything You I

In Anything You Put Your Mind To, *Liz uncovers one of the great secrets of success in both business and life: the potential of narrative to forge one's own path. People underestimate storytelling, but its power is infinite: the stories we tell ourselves constitute our reality.*

With verve and clarity, Anything You Put Your Mind To *brings home the importance of reconnecting with our stories, and demonstrates how anyone can follow Liz's lead and bring direction back to their self-narratives. The verities of this book—that the roads to every kind of both success and failure start inside our own heads—are striking, challenging, but ultimately liberating. Liz's account is searingly honest and her writing is compelling and lyrical. I loved how she skillfully manifests the clamoring forces we all internally wrestle with on a daily basis. Larry and the dog, the central characters of the book, are rendered with the weight and force of a fable. Every last word is heavy with the power of Liz's personal investment in her vision. No one else could have written this book.*

Anything You Put Your Mind To *will benefit anyone who wants to tell themselves better stories; that is, anyone who wants to change their life. Knowing which of our narratives to discard, which to alter, which to champion—this is the road to so much of what we call prosperity. This book is rich with the hard-won wisdom of one who has walked this road, and returned to tell the tale. Start reading. Now.*

— *AJ Leon, Founder of Misfit and author of*
The Life and Times of a Remarkable Misfit

There is no one like Liz Strauss. Liz is living insight, jumping over boundaries. Conversations with Liz are legendary for dizzying changes in perspective, unexpected connections, and bright ideas. This book is like a conversation with Liz, only portable. And more intense.

— *Becky McCray, Entrepreneur and author of* Small Town Rules

Liz Strauss is a world-renowned storyteller, so it is only fitting that she would use stories as both the framework and roadmap to help you to achieve success and everything that you want out of life. Whether you are an entrepreneur, a busy professional, or someone who's just asking, "what's next," Liz's unique, humorous, and insightful parable provides the perfect inspiration.

— *Carol Roth, Billion-dollar dealmaker, Judge on TBS's America's Greatest Makers, and author of the New York Times bestseller* The Entrepreneur Equation

Liz Strauss shares stories that illuminate who she is and at the same time will help you understand who you can become. This book will twist, bend, and batter your reality and that's a good thing. All of us need to make great leaps in our mind, and yours will start when you read the first chapter.

— *Tim Sanders, Author of* Love Is the Killer App: How To Win Business and Influence Friends

It would have been easy for Liz Strauss to pump out a business book. Or an inspirational book about conquering cancer. Or a series of ebooks on social media marketing.

Instead of taking the expected path, Liz zigged when she might have zagged. She's written a beautiful, jaw-droppingly original story that calls to mind Og Mandino, or perhaps Gabriel Garcia Marquez.

Her unique and incisive perspective shines through, hitting the reader right between the eyes by becoming fully vulnerable. If you've ever caught yourself "hiding in your thoughts," looking for human connection, or seeking to be understood, this book will become a treasured keepsake.

You'll understand what I mean when you read it. And you must read it.

— Rosemary O'Neill, Co-Founder, Social Strata

"Wouldn't that be cool?" Whenever I'd hear Liz Strauss utter those words, I knew I had just been given a gift from a dear friend—a tiny but yet oh so significant tidbit of wisdom that had been processed, analyzed, and delivered from one of the most brilliant minds I have, or will, ever encounter. So it was with great anticipation and pleasure that I dove into Liz's new book, Anything You Put Your Mind To.

It's a book that reveals the emotional and personal heart of this "65th Crayon"—a poignant and unflinching glimpse into a fertile and wondrous imagination, revealing rich textures of insight, wonder, and in the end, many simple truths we can take with us to guide and instruct our own lives.

She takes us on this personal journey with her "time machine"—a rich musical and lyrical accompaniment, a library of touching stories from her childhood, and two special friends—Larry and the dog.

And, there's the sky, where Liz gazes up and finds her place and part in the universe. The truths that she so eloquently notes ultimately leads to a larger life lesson—the way to find yourself is to look back, AND up—and just BE, with child-like curiosity and a reflective innocence.

Experience this wisdom yourself by reading this wonderful story, and then embark on your own journey of personal discovery. Wouldn't that be cool?

— Terry St. Marie, Portland, Oregon

A seemingly simple awakening of personal growth—set in modern day. Readers will meet the woman who is an "everyman": successful but unsure, loving yet controlling, happy and unbalanced, as well as righteously hypocritical. She is we.

The writer's distinguished intelligence and prose tell us her story in a wax-on, wax-off parable that is rich with clever insights and self-deprecating humor, which beckons the reader to relate and then question our own place in this world. All this is accomplished with introduction of a mysterious character named Larry and his dog.

As a reader, I cherished each word and chapter. This is a book you take your time with because, just like the main character, you will have to stop, pause, and listen to your inner voice. That voice might be telling you to address your buried Freudian issues, learn self-love, as well as how to give and receive, before you can enjoy your success.

Anything You Put Your Mind To will become the contemporary life-lessons business allegory for the 2010s; just like The Alchemist and The Legend of the Monk and the Merchant were for the late 90s and early 2000s. I will regularly pick this book up, again and again, to reread chapters, especially Liz Strauss' explanation of the "65th Crayon." I highly recommend this book for anyone who thinks they might be stuck, or who thinks that they already "have it all," or maybe they just want to reach further in their career.

—Jon-David, Author of 9 Amazon ebooks,
and a world-leading social media expert in the Salon Industry

It doesn't take long to recognize the truth behind Liz's recommendation, "Be curious about everything." In this dazzling, rippling adventure tale we are given the ride of a life. The secret ingredient propelling this story of stories is the thirst for knowledge driven by an unquenchable curiosity. Ever questing, Liz offers us a path to reflection and self-understanding both accessible and divorced from the step-driven, self-help of the past.

Through Liz's passion, her vision, and her unbridled willingness to explore we are offered a model for making and remaking ourselves.

For those who know Liz and her work, this is a welcome glimpse into "the Way of Liz" and offers revelations and surprises of all sorts. With wit she disarms and with wonder she instructs. All you have to do is keep up with this Alice in the wonderland that is her imagination.

— *Andrew [Drew] Marshall, CEO, Primed Consulting, LLC*

The best stories let you get lost in them and come out with new insights and actionable ideas; Liz creates that journey for you with this book. Liz has been an amazing friend and mentor for almost 10 years and I know that conversations with her can stretch your mind and open your eyes to opportunities you would have never seen otherwise. The sooner you read this book the sooner you can begin to live your new, exciting life stories.

—*Mark J. Carter, Founder of ONE80 and creator of Idea Climbing™*

An adventure in remembering
we decide the stories
that decide our lives

ANYTHING
You Put Your Mind To

Liz Strauss

with Foreword by Jane Boyd, Story Editor

GeniusShared Press

Delta, B.C.

Anything You Put Your Mind To by Liz Strauss

First published 2016 in Canada by GeniusShared Press, Delta, B.C.

Interior Design by: eBookDesignWorks.com

Cover Design by: Mark D'Antoni

Cover illustrations: Jackie Lea Shelley

Story Editor: Jane Boyd, GeniusShared Press

Creative Consultant: Richard Balkwill, CopyTrain

© 2016 M. E. Strauss. All rights reserved.

No part of this book may be reproduced in any written, electronic, recording, or photocopying without written permission of the publisher or author. The exception would be in the case of brief quotations embodied in the critical articles or reviews and pages where permission is specifically granted by the publisher or author.

Although every precaution has been taken to verify the accuracy of the information contained herein, the author and publisher assume no responsibility for any errors or omissions. No liability is assumed for damages that may result from the use of information contained within.

All reasonable efforts have been made to contact the copyright holders. Anyone who believes their copyright to be infringed is welcome to contact the publisher via email at geniusshared@gmail.com

Books may be purchased in quantity and/or special sales by contacting the publisher, GeniusShared Press at geniusshared@gmail.com.

Strauss, Liz, 1952—Anything You Put Your Mind To

ISBN 978-0-9951833-0-8 First Edition

    1. Self-Help, 2. Leadership, 3. Motivation

Printed in the United States

To my parents and family who started my story,
to my husband and son who gave it focus.
To them, my dear friends, my adversaries, and our experiences
which pushed me into a life of meaning.

Table of Contents

Stories About Stories

It was April. I had just made peace with the idea that my mom was dying of cancer when she called me crying to say that I needed to leave work immediately to make the 95 mile drive home. She'd chartered a plane and we were flying my dad to Mayo clinic.

At the Minnesota airport an ambulance whisked him off to the hospital. A taxi drove us to the rooming house across the street. I got my mom settled and talked her into a nap. I went to check on my dad. I arrived just in time to see him Code Blue and stood watching as the cardiac team got out the paddles that brought him back to life.

I was 26.

Paul waited tables at the tiny White House diner across the street from the hospital and next door to our rooming house. He was writing a book about Rochester, Minnesota, about how a city economy built on sickness changes people. I liked him. My mom liked him. It was nice to find a friend in this difficult situation.

Over time, things settled down. Paul became a welcome regular in our lives. When we were sure that my dad was in the clear, on one of his breaks, he invited me to take a walk. We talked about sickness and stress and he said, "You know what you need? You need to go kite flying!" And the next day we did.

As we flew kites we talked about what was happening with my parents. We named our kites and told stories about them. Then we started talking about what I hoped might happen in my own barely started life. We described a full-length movie of my life and on that day, we coined the motto, "It's my movie. I get to choose."

Anything You Put Your Mind To is an odyssey, a vision quest of how one person, with the guidance of true-hearted friends, examines the best true stories about her to claim and shape her life.

⇥ ⇥ ⇥

We all know that when people ask, we use stories to share who we are. We use stories to give a "one-minute bio" as we introduce one good friend to another. We use them to explain how accidents happen or how we came to make a mistake. Stories help us structure our life and give it meaning.

Recalling stories helps us understand our motives, and to identify experiences that prove I am like you. Stories stand as examples of what we're willing to share especially if what we're sharing is who we are.

It was the power of stories, both telling them and learning from them, that brought this book into being.

Most of us don't realize that if you reconsider a story you believe about yourself, shift your paradigm, retell it from a new point of view, you can change your life.

Stories can help us become who we want to be. The story about kite flying not only recalled an event but also changed my life. For some time after, I used that motto, "It's my movie. I get to choose." I used it to reconsider the stories I told about myself, to find a new way to see events, to own my actions until owning my life came naturally to me.

Our stories support or limit our success in business and in life. After kite flying, I began to question stories I told myself, especially stories I used to tell people who I am. Challenging my stories led me to challenge my beliefs about myself. Reconsidering one story, led me to understand that the world can't choose whether I belong, whether I have value. That decision is up to me.

This book is more than a story. It's a journey and a blueprint of how to reconnect with the stories you tell yourself so that you can make a simpler, easier, more meaningful life. Call it a quirky fantasy, a twisted memoir, or business parable. Whatever you call it, it's a great philosophy for finding success at work and in your life.

Liz Strauss
Author
Chicago, Illinois

Foreword

It was just over a year ago when Liz Strauss first sent me the manuscript of *Anything You Put Your Mind To.* She had written it several years prior and was considering publishing it. Liz asked me to read it and share my thoughts with her.

I still remember that on the day she sent it to me, she said "When you read this, it will explain a lot." Being a long time fan of the stories Liz tells and the words she writes, I was both curious and intrigued by what I would find in the manuscript.

I didn't realize it at the time, but I think Liz knew that I would also find the story to be incredibly helpful in my own life too.

I began reading the pages late at night, thinking I would get at least a few chapters in. Instead of doing that, I stayed awake the entire night and read the manuscript from beginning to end on my iPhone. To say it captured my mind, my heart and my attention all at once doesn't even begin to describe how I felt as I swiped from page to page in the darkness of the night. It was as if I was having a brain to brain and heart to heart conversation with my smartest, wisest and most caring friend. In retrospect, I guess I kind of was.

By the time I finished reading the sun was beginning to rise. I sat quietly trying to absorb the profound meaning of all I had just read. There was certainly something very special about the tale of Alice, Larry and the dog.

Two things were as clear as the light of day to me.

The first was that I realized that suddenly I was thinking about the stories inside my own head very differently. It was as though my perspective had been completely changed. To me, this was profound. For as long as I could remember, I had been working hard to outrun several very particular stories. They were the stories that caused me to doubt myself at the most inopportune moments, that held my voice hostage when it most wanted to speak up, and that interfered far too often with my self confidence. Sound familiar? Perhaps you have had a few of those stories in your head too.

The second was that I realized that this adventure in remembering—*about how we decide the stories that decide our lives*—had indeed explained a lot. It was as if I could suddenly see all the pieces to a puzzle—my own personal life puzzle.

Sitting there at 4:27 in the morning, I knew—as in *intuitively knew*—that this was THE book Liz was to publish. I was so certain about this that I wrote her an email that said:

> *"Reading this tonight has been like a gift. It helped me understand so much more—about so many different aspects of my life. Thank you for sharing it with me. There are so many things that I have sensed for so long—yet I just couldn't quite put it all together in a way that my mind could make sense of. You were so right when you said this story would explain a lot.*

This needs to be published! It's stunning in its truth, beauty and brilliance. This is a book about life. About work. About balance. And about relationships. It's all there—and then some. It's truly moving."

Many months later Liz asked me if I would take on the role of Story Editor for *Anything You Put Your Mind To*. I accepted immediately, finding myself once again curious and intrigued by what I would discover as we worked together to prepare the manuscript for publication.

Working with Liz on this book has given me the opportunity to dive deep into the way the stories in our head either limit or empower us. I have come to understand and appreciate why it's often so hard to know which stories we should pay attention to, which stories we should keep or throw away and which ones we should reframe.

Perhaps one of the biggest aspects of my role as the Story Editor has been to argue for you, the reader—for what you might think, experience, and feel as you make your way through the pages of this book. And for the insights that you will find yourself walking away with or coming to understand—even months after you have finished reading—being able to explore these issues as well as explain my own gut thinking to Liz has been both a growing and enlightening experience. Suffice to say, that finding clarity and being direct while standing in the thick of a story that is about the stories that are in your head proved to be something of an acquired skill.

Another area that I have worked closely with Liz on has been to make sure the characters remained true to themselves and that the events were as true to the story at the beginning as they were at the end. Alice, Larry and the dog are such unique and special characters—individually and collectively. I have loved getting to know them, spending time with them and seeing how they made story come together. I wanted to be sure you would find just as many reasons as Liz and I have to enjoy and appreciate them.

It has been an incredible experience to work with Liz on this book project. I am truly thankful to her for a multitude of reasons. I have learned so much about not only myself, business and relationships but about authoring and book publishing too. Liz is my business partner and one of my closest lifelong friends.

I believe you will find *Anything You Put Your Mind To* full of relevant and powerful insights that will enable you to do anything you put your mind to.

Jane Boyd
Story Editor
Delta, B.C.

Every story we tell is true, even stories
that didn't happen. Stories we tell about
ourselves are the most true of all.

—Liz Strauss

I went running today. I go running every day. Well, every day, except for the days I don't really feel like it.

On those days I go running twice.

Most people don't even suspect this about me. Most people are sure I've kept this six-foot skinny frame through the sheer luck of the gene pool and a severe lack of appetite. It's a reasonable assumption. After all, I don't eat much, and you'd be hard pressed to find someone who's actually seen me run—there's always another bus. *(Darn that Craig Capitani for saying I run like a girl.)*

You'd think that the perceptive ones might have picked up a clue from the fact that I love to drive my little car with the top down. If they had, they'd know I have this thing for the sky, especially in the wee hours of the night (or the morning) when there aren't many people around.

I've communed with the sky on four continents. It's like becoming part of a painting. Suddenly I become a perfect fit. The proportion of future and past wide open spaces matches the small tiny places where my feet touch the ground. Somehow I know exactly where I am in the universe, that God is in His heaven, and all is right with the world—my world, anyway.

And a good dose of sky is important, at times like these when the walls at work feel like they're closing in.

These days, I have the time to run. I'm on a medication that wakes me up too early to do anything else that this overthinking human usually does.

Now that I'm back in the city without my garden, rearranging the bark mulch outside of my building can cause an issue—even if I wait to do it when most people are sleeping. It draws unwelcome attention of the most disturbing kind. So I came to be a runner in the wee hours while the world's away. Besides, I look good in active wear—as long as it's not "needy pink."

I don't run along the paths. Actually, I don't run at all. I walk. Well, I walk, and sometimes I stand. Sometimes I move more like a three year old taking her body out on a test drive—walk a step or two; jump; jump. Dig in a heel, then the toes to see what happens; and jump again. Then get totally distracted by a blade of grass or a flower; and plop down to use my hands to check out where my feet have been.

Or I stop to stare at the sky for hours.

Or I lay myself down under a tree to see the leaves from the bottom up.

It's a peaceful and perfect way to start a day, except, of course, on the days that I just don't feel like it . . . which admittedly, are most days . . . especially if the weather is the least bit less than perfect . . . and maybe not at all when things at work are going less than perfectly. With this overthinking mind I can usually find a rationale to define any day that way—on those days, I go running in my mind.

It was on one of those "less than perfect days" that I first met Larry and the dog.

Chapter One

How I Met Larry
(and the dog)

THE MORNING I MET LARRY and the dog, the sky was
that backlit blue-black that stops time, tricking just about
everyone into thinking that morning is a long way off. The
moon had just left the scene and the sun had not yet made her
entrance. The birds were still sleeping. Couples soon to hook
up that Friday night were surely thinking they had plenty
of time to flirt their way to a bedroom or a back seat. More
serious folks tucked tightly in bed were waking to glimpse the
clock with one opened eye, and to roll back over with thoughts
of hours yet to sleep (or clutching frustrated thoughts of why
they couldn't sleep in the first place).

Me? I was enjoying the luxury of time—time to sit smack dab
in the middle of a slow moving transition. For the next little

bit I could do, or be, or see whatever I wanted. I had time—time to see the colors in the sky—time to go running through the pathways of my mind.

On this particular day, I didn't have to rationalize some less than perfect weather. Though the temperature was a perfect 74 degrees on Mr. Fahrenheit's scale, my pressure-sensitive head told me that you could touch the humidity in the air. Even the lowest roadie on a rock tour would have called it a bad hair day.

The weather inside my head wasn't perfect either. My mind was under a tornado warning. My boss, Benny, once my biggest fan, had undergone an inexplicable change of heart. Now he kept touching down in my office, causing chaos and making up rules to keep me on my computer and not interacting with my team. Inmates at the state correctional facility were enjoying their work duties more than I was. Every thought of going to work made me think of ways to escape.

So, I prepared for my run. I put on my lightweight indigo active wear and my black and purple trim running shoes—which had yet to feel the harsh feedback of actual pavement. I pulled on my denim and khaki City of San Francisco ball cap from the sailing trip I took with Charlene.

A quick check in the mirror found me thinking it appropriate that the blue of the suit and that of my eyes tied nicely to the indigo color of the sky.

I set my headphones—yes, the big black headphones—to something ironic and took off running. To be accurate, I sat back in my favorite chair. I mentally made my way out of the building, across Lake Shore Drive to the shore of the lake.

You already know that I didn't run—the original "bus logic" applies here too—the lake wasn't going anywhere.

Still, in my mind I was flying! Everywhere east was water and sky. Everywhere above was sky. Everywhere west was fabulous architecture—Louis Sullivan facades, a 17th century Cotswold manor house, the Piazza Unità in Trieste, and a chandelier I remembered from a dream. Everywhere north, including where I worked, was behind me.

I made my way to a wise and welcoming oak tree in a quiet corner of Lincoln Park. It stood out in my memory, because I had cleverly imported it from the backyard of my childhood some 90 miles away.

That's one of the perks of running my way, I get to pick the details. . . . And this was some detail . . . an 80-foot white oak with a trunk about three feet in diameter. It must have been at least 90 years old and showed every sign of living at least 200 years more.

At that point in my run, I had reached the intersection of Left Brain and Right. Language lives Left, and life there was that of an adrenaline junkie, a workaholic pulled thin as a wire, unable to rest. Colors, patterns, mathematics live to the Right, as does my soul. I chose Right, which was only right.

I settled in under that friendly and familiar majestic oak tree and pulled up a handful of grass from my childhood backyard right there in Lincoln Park.

I watched the grass change shape in the humidity, slowly curling into beautiful shapes—as opposed to what my hair might have done in that same situation. Memories of humid days gone by immediately came flooding back, in their own sticky way. In minutes, they morphed into memories of me in gardens past. There I was digging up dirt so dry you had to wet it to make dust or laying bark mulch as I solved problems or conflicts at work.

I stopped to consider the incredible amount of plants and supplies I had transported in the tiny cars I had always owned. I was moved by these memories to compose an ode to peat moss and humus, wondering as I did whether Shakespeare had ever written a drunken poem to shit in the wee hours of the morning.

> *An Ode to Humus*
> *Gone the peat, No more the loam*
> *Lo, I've left the gardens' home*
> *Here no humus sweetens air*
> *Sticking clumps not anywhere*
> *'Fore the buildings stand the plants*
> *Small then gone, they might be ants*
> *That the people see no more,*
> *As they run through building's door*
> *But alas! Were I to stand*
> *I'd feed each bloom from my own hand*
> *Gently, kindly, I'd be forsworn*
> *From this duty, ne'er to be torn*
> *Do not try me, nor defy me*
> *Flowers tease and mystify*
> *Each small flower I would treat*
> *With the taste of pure humus sweet.*

Having thus fulfilled my literary yearning, I leaned back to fill my eyes with sky. Leaving the words behind, I considered how I might spend more time exercising the right side of my brain. For me, the left was about rules, and structure, and grammar; the right was about freedom, and expression, and music. If I was looking for balance giving time to my right brain seemed a good place to start. How does one offer a balanced diet to one's brain?

> *Be curious about everything. Don't overthink anything.*
> *Take an equal dose of color for every word you see, hear, or say.*
> *Try to think more about less.*

That last thought led me to thinking about what fun it is to think about nothing, and how long it had been since I'd done that except in cases where my brain just shut down. I thought about how people around me seemed to look for ways not to think, or at least look for more ways to think about nothing.

I'd been sitting there thinking thoughts about thinking about thinking nothing. Don't get me wrong. At that moment, I wasn't thinking about nothing. I was thinking about what people do to think about nothing—things like gardening, golfing, meditating, watching TV, until eventually I actually was thinking about nothing. I suppose, I was doing something like meditating—in a mind-running sort of way—just letting my thoughts sit out in the color of the sky. Until I heard a voice. . . .

"Do you think it's a good idea to be out here on a bad hair day sitting under an imported majestic backyard tree when the sky is tricking everyone into thinking that morning is a long way off?" this intruding voice said.

"Huh?" I replied, pulled from my thoughts out there in the colors of the sky, to figure out how a guy and a dog got into my private, right-brain run through Lincoln Park.

"Sorry to startle you," replied this oversized sixth-grader of what I guessed to be about 40-something, "I just wanted to make sure you were safe."

"Safe? Safe? Are you crazy?" I answered in total disbelief. "I'm running in my head. What could possibly happen to me in my head?"

"My point exactly," he said. "There are places inside your head that are considered some of the most perilous places on the planet. Think about it. You should know. You live in that head. Unless, of course, you've become complacent."

"Who are you?" I demanded. "And while we're at it, who is he?" I'm not sure how I knew the dog was a he, but I knew he was.

All of my life I've just known things—sort of just picked up information from the air. At this moment that skill was particularly engaged.

"I'm Larry," the man with banana hands said, with a Dennis Quaid glint in his eye, "and that's the dog."

"The dog, you call him 'the dog?' Not even 'Dog' with a capital 'D'? That doesn't seem right." I asked this in amazement. I used to teach first grade. "Did you guys just meet?"

"No," Larry said as he brought the big dog's face to his own, giving the dog a first-class scratch behind both ears, "we've been hanging out together for a number of years."

"I see. Well, if you're such close companions, why doesn't 'the dog' have a proper name?" I inquired.

"Oh, he probably does." Larry said patiently. "He just hasn't shared it with me."

I took that moment to take in the sky, which during our discourse had begun to lighten considerably. I was filled with feelings—fury, impatience, a touch of an unnamed fear, and a cash load of curiosity. In my most grown-up persona, I decided to let it go and return to what I had been doing. But, despite my sincere attempts to throw my thoughts back into the colors of the sky, the sky remained there. And my thoughts remained with me and Larry and the dog.

My frustration wasn't that different from those folks clutching tightly to their pillows at not being able to get back to sleep.

I could not return to what I had been doing, because I had a super-sized man and his no-name dog sitting with me inside my head waiting patiently for me to pay attention to them.

This was a real problem.

I had taken up running to avoid just this kind of thing.

> *Some people don't see it, but I was born with a double dose of the self-conscious gene. I take self-consciousness to an art form, particularly when people I don't know are waiting for me. Triple that when the people I don't know who are waiting for me are watching me as they wait. Cube the response when they are waiting patiently.*

Within milliseconds, I'm picturing both Larry and the dog tracking my hair as it grows, one follicle at a time. Darn if each follicle isn't taking its own sweet time to grow in the most inappropriate fashion. I can feel every follicle giving away the exact location of each of my most personal secrets, including the time I convinced a boy that I was twins AND the time that I stood on the table in kindergarten and sang "The Good Ship Lollipop," as if I were Elvis Presley.

They were looking at me and waiting—patiently. It was excruciating.

I could hardly bear it. It felt like fingernails on chalkboards plus a dentist's drill plus a baby crying on an airplane plus your significant other saying "You're not going to wear that, are you?" happening while your boss is giving you a new and complicated project due in twenty minutes just as the fire alarm in your building goes off.

I tried to block it. I tried to ignore it. I tried to lose myself in the sky. I tried to crawl back into my head in order to go back to thinking about thinking about not thinking. But the noise of their watching and waiting was too distracting and too disconcerting. I was desperate.

So I broke out in song.

> *I've been through the desert with a dog with no name*
> *It felt good to be out of the rain*
> *In the desert you can remember your name*
> *'Cause there ain't no one for to give you no pain.*
> *La, La, La, La, La, La, La.*[1]

I figured that those few lines from the America song "Horse with No Name" might work much as it had in college when I sang "Red River Valley" for two hours until Susie Browne finally caved in and told me to stop. If nothing else, it might serve to distract the distractors. But that superhero of a dog was too much for me. He merely sidled over, plopped his big head in my lap, and offered me a wide-eyed stare that said *Who do you think you're fooling?*

I choked. I swallowed. I felt like I should apologize to a dog.

"Okay, okay," I whispered. "I surrender." I was defeated by that dog's caramel eyes. I'm sensitive to color.

There was more to this dog than Larry was letting on.

I found myself starting to think as though I knew Larry and to consider what he had said about seeing whether I was safe. Suppose I had wandered into some treacherous place in my own head? He was right. I did live there and I wasn't willing to state unequivocally that it wasn't possible.

> **HEADLINE NEWS:** *Woman Meets Chainsaw Killer and Dog in Back Alleys of Her Own Head. Tune in Tonight at 11.*

Not a pretty thought.

I resolved to return to riding the colors of the sky and to thinking about thinking about not thinking. I imagined a musical score for the occasion.

The truce held. We all sat back to enjoy what was now sunrise in full bloom. It was soft. It was soothing. It was something. Suddenly the sky was everything a little girl could ask for. Yep. *This* was what I had gone running for.

Ever since I could remember, this event filled me with faith, hope, and joy every time. I have to admit, it was kind of nice to have a couple of cohorts nearby who were seeing it too. It changes the experience of a sunrise nicely in some way.

I switched the score to something elegantly simple and reminded myself that I should edit the balance rule to include not only an equal dose of color for every word, but also twice as much music.

> *Be curious about everything. Don't overthink anything.*
> *Take an equal dose of color and twice the music for every word*
> *you see, hear, or say. Try to think more about less.*

It had been woefully remiss of me. As the younger sister of two card-carrying baby boomers, to have forgotten to include music from the start.

> *My brothers, much like all baby boomers, have a thing for music. It's because boomers fervently believe they grew up with the best music of all time. The unparalleled wealth and richness of the music of the 60s and 70s has screwed up their worldview. It has set the bar for their standards in life. They believe everything should be that good. That's why they get cranky and disappointed so easily. When boomers get that way, just put on some music.*

I wondered whether Larry and the dog could hear the music playing in my head. I worried whether they would appreciate my choice if they could. Then I figured they were too young to know this stuff. Sad.

"Yeah, that would've been our choice too. We're big fans. We're older than we look, you know," Larry informed me, just as I noticed the gray at his temples. The dog made it clear that Larry wasn't joking.

"My apologies, I didn't mean to be thinking so loudly," I remarked, and simultaneously adjusted my perceptions to include a man with an age over 40 and a dog with an uncanny ability to make things clear. That done, I questioned why I was apologizing for thinking, when it was they who had interrupted me. I was doing just fine thinking about thinking about not thinking before they found their way into my head.

"No worries. In any case, we wandered by to see what you were up to. But you never did say. What are you doing out here on a bad hair day sitting under an imported tree when the sky is tricking everyone into thinking that morning is a long way off?"

"Gosh," I said, "I'd love to tell you, but morning's no longer a long way off. Please forgive me. I don't usually go running after sunrise, especially on a bad hair day when I have to get to work . . . and I really can't afford to be late or screw things up in any way."

And being one who's never been very good at transitions, I sort of stumbled off like a bashful, distracted three-year-old test-driving her body, pulling the majestic tree from my childhood behind me. Larry and the dog didn't seem to mind.

In fact, I'm not sure they even noticed.

Chapter Two

It's Saturday, You Fool

I OPENED MY EYES and sat up at my desk, my backyard tree forlorn and forgotten. I removed my headphones, shook my head for a second and turned the playlist off. I have no clue why I had to get out of there so quickly. I'm not usually one to panic in such situations, but this one was weirder than I am. And that's a pretty good barometer of knowing when it's time to go.

Someone, two someones, so to speak, had just knocked my marbles off my tray. What to do now? I wasn't about to close my eyes again. They very well might still be there. I was too agitated for a simple, serene, and mindful run anyway. Movement. I needed movement.

I needed air. I couldn't sit still. It was time for a real walk in the real world with real people. I needed to find my feet.

No thinking about it necessary. I was outside the building in no time.

Somehow getting my feet moving under the sky and having the chance to touch a real-world tree or two—not to mention avoiding the occasional small child attempting to steer a two-wheeler for the first time—got my brain working. I began to feel some semblance of control returning.

On the first quarter of the walk, I questioned the ethics of a guy and a dog who would intrude on the running of my mind. Half way around, I realized they hadn't done anything but look in on me and share a sunrise. By the time I was on the third leg, I realized I'd enjoyed having company while the colors were changing. I'd even admitted that they added interesting variety to an average morning. By the time I had turned back into my building, I was sure that I had settled the issue as a minor jiggle in the structure of my life.

Or not. Would that it had been settled so easily.

I headed for the elevator and pushed the button for the 18th floor. That's when I suddenly had to admit how much my interaction with Larry and the dog had thrown me—I don't live on the 18th floor. When the doors opened on what was not my floor, I said hello and smiled to Mini-Cooper girl, the non-smiling, twenty-something who does. She boarded the lift to head down to the garage and I rode with her down to my own floor. She didn't notice I seemed to have joined the elevator-riding club for that day.

To our Mini-Cooper girl most people were invisible, so my secret blunder stayed nonexistent in her reality. Which begs the question:

If a woman rides an elevator to the wrong floor but eventually gets out on the right floor when no one is there to see her mistake, is there a sound?

I had hoped that ridiculously unrelated question would have triggered a string of similar stupid questions to distract me from my encounter with my new acquaintances, but such was not to be my fate.

As I turned the key to the safety of my homestead, strains of the "William Tell Overture" and words from my childhood began playing relentlessly through my mind. I heard the voiceover from The Lone Ranger. I saw the masked man on his mighty horse, Silver, riding off into the sunset as someone asked, "Who was that masked man?"

The tape in my head was stuck in a loop, "Who was that masked man?" But I was thinking about my encounter with a stranger and his dog in the corners of my mind. I was pretty sure that this time the answer was not the Lone Ranger. I had a feeling Tonto, his sidekick, wasn't going to be of much help either.

It was about this time I realized I didn't have to go to work. A giant billboard in my head read

It's Saturday, you fool.

Banana-hand Larry and his caramel-eyed, make-it-clear dog had sparked an unhinging effect on my equilibrium. My feet decided they needed to *not* do something, so that I could get myself back together.

I needed a chance to sort things out. I needed a new view, a new route for my mind. I went back to my desk and sat down.

I pulled on my headphones and prepared to go running in an open mind.

I chose Lyle Lovett's "If I Had a Boat." I sat back and joined him with his pony on his boat. I figured it was a safe bet that no one named Larry would bring his no-name dog to bother me while I was listening to a story Mr. Lovett wrote about being out the ocean with the Lone Ranger and a pony on a boat. And if by some chance they did, Mr. Lovett's pony could help me outrun them.

And it worked . . . for a while. I hid in my mind for a while, contemplating the ocean, the pony, and the boat.

Quietly real world thoughts started creeping in. My mind switched to remembering what I was supposed to do on this particular Saturday that I had mistaken for a Monday after a chance meeting with an overgrown 6th grader and his lowercase 'd' dog.

Ack! Tonight was Richard Gabinski Bumgartner Smith's "going away to *not* join the army" party. He would be leaving us in the early morning to direct *La Traviata* at an American Army Base in Germany.

I was invited as Richard's identical twin, because we look so much alike—except that he has black hair and brown eyes and is a guy, and I have blonde hair and blue eyes and am not . . . a guy. *(But then you knew that.)*

The entire Boystown community was putting together the sendoff of the year for Evil Uncle Richard. The celebration, which promised to include bawdy show tunes, bad Shakespeare, and plenty of shiny windmill drink stirrers from Richard's last birthday party, was a private event open only to thirty or so of Richard's most entertaining friends dressed in character.

Just as suddenly I was in the music and back on the boat again. But I knew I needed to return to the real world to get ready for the party. So as Mr. Lovett was finishing his set, I jumped to the deck—me upon my pony upon my boat—and together woman on pony on boat headed for home to get done up for the party. No time now for thinking about thinking about not thinking. *(Maybe I can't walk on water, but thank God that a pony on a boat can.)* We crossed Lake Shore Drive without event.

As I dismount and step out of the boat, I inadvertently glance down at my running shoes, noticing the first marks of the pavement marring their pristine attractiveness.

> *Note to Self: Write Mr. Lovett to say that we'll be needing very tall ponies from now on, because he and I both have legs too long to be riding normal ponies on boats without scuffing our shoes in the process.*

And lo, at that very moment the heavens part, great chords of music begin playing, and the voice of my mother calls down from above to say, "While you're at it, remind yourself and that Lovett boy not to stop your bikes by dragging the toes of your shoes either. Shoes cost good money."

My mom. She thinks I know everyone.

I sent off the pony and boat to the stable and dry dock respectively. Then with the insouciant air of one who has all of the time in the world, including yours, I entered the building. I chattered a cheerful hello to the door staff and found my way up the elevator—this time to the right floor on the very first try.

> *Score one for the little girl in the indigo active wear, who navigates the world better in her own mind.*

As the door shut behind me, though, I took off my headphones and returned to the real world.

Hmmm. As I thought about my costume, the evil me started to wonder should I be Larry or should I be the dog? But in the end, respect for my evil twin, Richard, took over and Alice in Wonderland prevailed. I could do Alice and I had the perfect shoes for it.

Besides Larry and the dog don't count as characters, because nobody had heard of them but me, and now you, but you weren't going to the party.

I became dervishly obsessed with becoming Alice. I pulled out my white poet's blouse and my perfectly blue dress. I began obsessing about how to Alicessorize it.

I grabbed the shoes that were born for this occasion. They not only look 17th century with their clunky heels and squared-off toes, but also for a pair that have been life mates, they have always been not quite the same shade of brown-black—a quality I find endearing and which has brought us closer together as a family of shoes and person.

The apron. What do I do about the apron?

> *Who believed Alice ever did anything useful in*
> *the kitchen anyway? She was the daughter of*
> *the Dean of Christ Church, a college at Oxford.*
> *What was the big deal about the darn apron?*
> *Most people don't notice that the apron is often a*
> *square at the top, a bib like bib overalls, with no*
> *straps to hold it up—now how was I supposed to*
> *pull that off?*

Digging through past lives I had squirreled away in my condo, I got to the one called "World's Greatest Seamstress," which really meant the person who has the most fabric wins.

I had moved this particular past life from Austin to Boston to Chicago just for this occasion, it seems. For there was the answer I sought—11 yards of white fabric, lovely linen and rayon blend, lightweight, yet practical, which would be charming with any ensemble.

Just because I'm that way, I took a moment to go online to check my facts and was relieved to find that the safety pin was available on the planet at about the same time as Alice was.

I wasn't going to quibble over whether she personally had any. I figured she must have—I remind you, she was the daughter of the Dean. On the other hand, they were probably prized possessions and she was one of three daughters. Being one of three siblings myself, I know the possibility that her siblings might have decided that they needed her safety pins more.

In any case, at that moment the more important issue was not whether Alice Liddell had any safety pins, but whether or not I did.

The search began. First the drawers: in desks, in the bathrooms, in the kitchen, in the file cabinet drawers where the pencils are. I opened; I saw; I found none. Then several cases: suitcases, make-up cases, briefcases, computer cases. Again I looked; I saw; I found none. I was reduced to my closet, checking my dry cleaning for glimpses of shiny metal, like some manic crow.

Filled with both resentment and gratitude upon finding exactly two safety pins, I both cursed and thanked the cleaners, because I hate it when they hang my pants with safety pins, and on too many occasions I have asked them not to.

It only took about 3 hours and 24,635 minutes to fold and pin that 11 yards of white fabric—lovely linen and rayon blend, lightweight, yet practical, which would be charming with any ensemble—into the perfect Alice apron. It took so long because naturally, any day now, I might take up sewing again and want to make something out of that 11 yards of white fabric, lovely linen and rayon blend, lightweight, yet practical, which would be charming with any ensemble. Also the blue dress I was pinning it to buttoned up the front, so I had to pin the makeshift apron on the dress while the dress was on me. Let's just say thinking about thinking about not thinking is easier than pinning on something on something on someone.

But finally I was ready to go the party and couldn't wait to see what characters beyond Evil Uncle Richard I would get to see.

Chapter Three

The Problem with Parties

I WAS READY TO GO ALL RIGHT. I closed my eyes and went through a checklist of beyond-the-call-of-duty details to verify.

I had raided my "Great Seamstress" past life a second time to find the perfect one-inch-wide, heavenly-blue satin ribbon for my hair. Check.

I had sought out my "I Think I'll Act Like a Girl This Year" past life—admittedly that life had lasted a mere two hours—to find my wireless curling iron to do the "do" as Alice would do. Check.

I had gone on to raid my "First Grade Teacher of the Millennium" past life to locate a bedraggled, stuffed white rabbit to serve as my date and my personal security from conversations with people who have no imagination. Check.

And, not to be discounted, I was fully equipped with the confidence that comes from having completed the act of pinning something on something on someone, which was harder than thinking about thinking about not thinking. Check plus.

The make-up was perfect Alice. The mindset was perfect party. I knew I could handle this party with finesse and charm, and that I would enjoy doing so. Check and double check.

A large lowercase 'd' appeared in my mind's eye.

I had just finished mentally checking off that last "I can handle this with party finesse and charm," when a pair of caramel-no-name-dog eyes appeared in my thoughts. The eyes in question intended to make it clear that neither the lowercase 'd' dog nor I, myself, really believed that my statement "I can handle this party . . . " was anywhere near reality.

Caught acting by a specter of a no-nonsense dog.

I mentally returned to my list. Erase check with double check. Strike through and add a minus.

Caramel-eyes challenged my thoughts: Why do you insist on trying to fool yourself into thinking such things?

Great, tell me something I don't know.

> *Note to Self:* Tell dog that if he's going to edit my thinking and not share his name, he should, at the very least, initial his work.

Ready for the party—or not, in the dog's opinion—my work here was done. I was physically, if not mentally, set to go. Unfortunately the party was not ready for me—or anyone else for that matter. Guests were not invited for at least two hours. Maybe I'd have been better off if today really was Monday.

The brief thought of work made me cringe.

Renowned for my ability to turn on a dime, I focused my chameleon-like, paradigm-changing skills on the plot line of my next two hours. I'd use the time to get into character. It took seconds to find what I needed in my entry hall bookshelves. It was appropriately set with like content three shelves down and four shelves over. As I lifted the beautiful volume from its place, I appreciated that this single book and the memories it held could both distract and entertain me for any block of time.

> *Note to Self:* Take time to run through the library of your life.

I sat at my desk with a first edition of *Alice in Wonderland*. It had been a gift from a college friend who still calls me Alice. I was ready to spend some time in what Dr. Seuss so aptly named "The Waiting Place."

I felt the cover and reminisced. Each page was packed with memories of first, second and multiple encounters with the characters in the story, including that mad pack of theater people in college who had become my family. We had put together a rare and creative *Alice in Wonderland* for the stage.

❖   ❖   ❖

I became a "theater person" by accident, or maybe by argument, one very hot, early September night my sophomore year. I had been out to get a hot ham and cheese sandwich from the sub shop next door to the campus theater. On my way, I stopped in the open doorway to watch auditions. The sign said, "Open auditions for Alice in Wonderland, *an original production performed by an ensemble cast."*

My feet were stuck on the pavement. My eyes went to the stage. I couldn't enter the building, but I couldn't leave. I resigned myself to eat standing in the doorway.

Some freshman was reading for Alice. She was short for her body and said her lines like a first grader learning to read with expression. It hurt to listen. I remembered thinking, "I'm sure her intent is good, but this is no Alice. This is a dormouse. Let her sleep and give someone else a shot."

I watched four or five more Alice wannabes and was left wondering how they would find an Alice. I saw no curiosity, no child testing her limits. It was wrong, just WRONG. Alice was smart, savvy, and brave. These college girls acted as if anyone under 13 was stupid, naïve, and afraid.

(Which was an interesting counterpoint to the advice of the times, "Don't trust anyone over 30.")

Sandwich long forgotten, I was compelled to audition then and there.

After the audition, I approached the director, handed over my info sheet, and said, "Do you have a problem with a 6-foot Alice, who's not a theater major?"

"No," was all he said.

I got the part.

I got a family of friends and an encyclopedia of experiences along with it.

⇥⇤ ⇥⇤ ⇥⇤

I reflected on how it seemed fitting that a hot ham and cheese sandwich would trigger a turning point in my life. Fitting, remarkable, and inspiring. My life changed. My circle of friends changed. My way of interacting with the world changed. The Alice event had influenced me. I had become curiouser and curiouser.

My friend Peg says I'm the most curious person she knows. I often ask whether that means I ask a lot of questions or that I'm really strange. Her answer is always, "See?"

My curiosity has taught me all that I know.

I checked the clock—plenty of time before the party. I returned to the volume in my lap. I paged through *Alice*, stopping on my favorite drawings by Tenniel—the falling Alice, the BIG and little Alice, the grin without a cat, and the Mad Hatter's Tea Party. That illustration stopped me cold.

The tea party brought reeling home everything I know about parties. I closed the book and closed my eyes.

Larry and the dog were staring back at me. My eyes flew open again. I looked at the stuffed penguin on my bookcase. My breathing returned. I was a dormouse.

I couldn't think about the two beings behind my eyelids. I had more immediate fish to fry. Larry or no Larry, the dog was right. I wasn't ready to handle party animals with or without finesse and charm. Alice and I had to get into Cheshire cat mode or we wouldn't make it through this party whole. It was a good thing we were bringing the rabbit. This was no simple Mad Hatter's Tea Party.

Parties are part zoo, part lion's den, and part Serengeti for me. The self-conscious gene kicks in and wearing a costume is only more self-conscious making. Parties, like most other experiences in life, would be so much less complicated if there weren't other people involved.

The problem with parties is that people who go to them don't start out in agreement about almost anything about the party. Some are there because they want to meet people; some because they haven't anything better to do; some because they think the party is real life; some because they want to get away from real life. Cyndi Lauper says, "Girls just want to have fun." Try to get a definition of fun that two people agree on. That's just one example.

> *I had fun once. I don't remember if it was at a party. Usually I can't tell if I've had fun at a party until sometime the next day.*

So there I sat holding Alice's storybook in my lap, trying to sort party questions. Do I go early and wait for the fun to start? Do I go later and try to catch up once the fun has started? What if I get there and the fun is over? How will I know when I have had enough fun to leave? The parties in my head are so much easier to deal with.

Forgetting my earlier experience, I closed my eyes.

Before I could snap them open again, Larry said, "Do you think it might be within the realm of possibility that you—or your friend Alice—could be overthinking this party thing?"

"You again," I said, attempting disregard, but feeling grateful for a sounding board. "Well yes, I suppose I am blowing this a little out of proportion."

"Aren't you the one who tells everyone that there are angels everywhere? That people are just waiting for a chance to be generous?" Larry wasn't pulling any punches. He wasn't being mean either.

"Guilty as charged," I admitted.

"So, why is it so hard for people to take their own advice?"

I had him on that one. "Because we're people." I threw in, "we're supposed to be a pain. You know, like Ben Franklin said, 'Things that hurt instruct.' I'm just being a hot stove."

The dog looked me straight in the eye as if to say *No, you had it right the first time; you're just being a pain.*

"How do you know so much about me, Mr. Larry who lives in my head?" I challenged. "How do you know that I tell people about angels and letting other people be generous?"

"That hurts," Larry answered back. "You're the one who told me about people wanting to be generous. You're the one who introduced me to the dog. You're the one who introduces everyone to everyone."

"I know you? How do I know you? Talk to me." I needed to know more and he was starting to talk.

"Can't talk now. You have a party to go to, Alice," was all that he said.

"Come to the party with me. You can bring your companion, the dog." I said with more sarcasm than I had intended.

The dog's face let me know he was thinking *You're better than that.*

Larry simply stated, "Nope, can't go to the party. We have plans and you need to send off your friend on your own. But you'll see us both sooner than you think."

In a blink, I lost sight of them. I can't say if they walked out the door, faded to black, or popped like a balloon, but I knew they were gone. I literally felt their absence, too.

Still, I prize irony especially when it happens inside my own mind. I found a lovely irony here. To think—I had been turned down for a non-date to a real-life party by a non-person and his lowercase 'd' non-dog because they had other plans. This hit me as an experience worth noting.

> *The way I figure it: all new experiences are worth noting. The ones that give you a good story are worth having. Those that leave great pictures in your head are priceless. This one had been all three.*

I held that priceless picture in my mind. The picture of how Larry and the dog left me was a colorized, black and white photo greeting card. It showed a poor, homeless, little Alice-waif looking tattered and bothered, holding a bedraggled, broken-down, stuffed white rabbit. The caption read *The rabbit and I have had a little talk about punctuality.*

A quick reality check showed that the sky was still light, but fading. The weather app on my phone showed a 40 percent chance of rain. Good news. Despite the unseasonably warm weather, I had an excuse to wear a raincoat. Though I found my Alice-wear quite becoming, it was not my first choice for ways to attract attention while crossing town. I'm more of an indigo active-wear woman.

The reality check also placed the earliest time of departure at least an hour away. The L & d experience had led me to set aside fantasy for now. I pushed *Alice in Wonderland* over to the side of my desk. To fill this hour and to fill my head, I sought a composition book I think of as "Mostly Poor Poetry from My Youth," inside a thick file of personal writing. To find this file, I knew I would have to look in one of three places.

Somehow it seems that everything I own must be located by looking in one of three places. Naturally, it's not the same three places for each thing. Shoes have three distinctively different places from safety pins, which have three distinctively different places from a writing pad I might be looking to find.

> *This is a hard concept for high-structure people to get their heads around. In fact, as I type this, I can feel my high-structure mom telepathically sending vehement messages from heaven to say, "if you would put things away you would know where to find them." But in this case, mom, that's just not the point. Anyone who's ever tried to organize a box of 64 crayons knows that everything on earth has more than one right place to be.*
>
> *High-structure people tend to be linear in their thinking and unfortunately not everything on the earth can be organized in a linear fashion. Think about the crayons. When you sort the crayons, do you put the blue violet crayon with the blues or the violets? And if you do, how does that affect where you put the red violet or the blue green? If you put the red violet with the reds, your violets will be incomplete, but if you put it with the violets, your reds will. You would need at least two, maybe three boxes of 64 crayons to organize your crayons this way properly. (I think this might be why Peg says I think in "656 nested ifs.")*

If you look at the world in a serial, but non-linear fashion, everything has three basic places where it rightfully belongs—with the stuff like itself, with the stuff it gets used with, and in the place where it gets used. Three perfectly viable places where it could, should, or would belong. Any one of them is a reasonable place to keep it.

As I went through three places to find the right folder and the three parts of the folder to a particular poem, I relived how this folder got its name.

⋯ ⋯ ⋯

I was in my "write to get my feelings out" stage. I had a problem throwing away my "bad, awful, no good, terrible, I know they stink yet I can't revise them" attempts at poetry. In fear that I might die, and made paranoid by children's books with "a someone reads your diary" plot, I wanted to feel safe that no one would ever think that I thought these attempts were poetry. So, on the rarest of chance that someone should stumble across them and for some stupid reason actually read them, I labeled certain writings: Good, Fair, or Poor. The word is written in pencil, should I change my mind—I never will. I knew that then. I still haven't thrown them away. I can't.

⋯ ⋯ ⋯

I tell myself I still keep those early pages to remind me how young young can be. Everyone needs such things around. They keep us human. Maybe one day I'll be human without them. Then I'll pay someone to sneak into my house and throw those awful poems away for me. Unfortunately I can't throw away awful old photos either. So I guess I'll be looking for a two-for-one.

That poetry-chasing quest took about fifteen minutes. I found the right folder and placed it on my desk. I found the poem, pushed the folder aside, and placed the poem on my desk.

The poem in question was one I'd written for a boyfriend in college. It perfectly fit the way I was feeling these many years later. Not that I had b-friend feelings for Larry. I didn't even know him. It was just that Larry and the 'd' were beginning to take up space in my head.

The fact that the two drifters seemed free to come and go in my head whenever they pleased didn't seem fair. Instead of thinking about thinking about not thinking, I was thinking about L and lowercase 'd', and that was bothering me. I didn't like it that I was thinking about Larry and the dog when, at the very least, I could be bored waiting for the time when I could leave for the party.

I read the poem. I read it again. I wrote it down in my very best handwriting. Writing it down reset my balance.

> **Bother**
> *Bother: to annoy, worry, or perplex*
> *There are days that*
> *I refuse to let people bother me*
> *And so I pass my time*
> *Involved in more constructive things*
> *I sew*
> *I sleep*
> *I write endless letters to people*
> *I hardly know*
> *I try to read books or magazines*
> *or even yesterday's newspaper*
> *I make myself a sandwich.*
> *And then I find myself*
> *—annoyed, because I want to hear an explanation*
> *—worried, because there may not be one*
> *—and perplexed, because I really don't understand*
> *what's going on*

And still
I sit
refusing to let people* bother me

*or their lowercase 'd' dogs

I read the poem over several more times and ended up feeling no longer alone or bothered. My emotional bank account was renewed for any necessary withdrawals. I was ready to greet the night.

As I set the poem on top of its folder, I swear I heard a lowercase "yip" of approval in the background—but they were gone. Weren't they?

Oh well, I wasn't about to be bothered thinking about that now. I had a party to attend, and finally it was time to go.

I headed out the door and to the elevator.

Chapter Four

Get this Party Started

I WALKED RIGHT UP TO the elevator, reached right out to the button, and turned right around. An unbiased observer might have thought it part of a dance routine for how fluid the movement was executed. Would that it were. As it happened, when the time finally arrived that the party was ready for me, I was no longer ready for the party. I had left Richard Gabinski Bumgartner Smith's "going away to *not* join the army" party gift back in the condo.

Does everything in life come down to timing? Well no, most of life is paying attention, but I'll save that discussion. Now it's time to get the party started.

I deftly re-entered the condo. Feeling like a schoolmarm at the sound of my wood heels on wood floors, this ex-teacher went straight to the package I had gathered and wrapped weeks ago for this event. Quick about face, and soon I was reaching for the elevator button again—this time actually making contact.

The doors opened to reveal Mini-Cooper girl herself—again. Damn if I didn't have the most blissful timing. I couldn't help but be in a cheerful mood imagining her response to what I held in my arms. *Ah, young Ms. Mini. May I call you Mini? How scandalized would you be if you had a clue of what was in this box?* With a rebellious imagination running wild, I flash her my most wooing smile and cheerfully attempt a conversation.

"Good evening. What luck to see you again so soon," I said cheerfully, feeling protected by the secret of my box and the white rabbit that is half in and half out of the pocket of my raincoat. Keeping her unbroken record, Mini-Cooper girl said NOTHING.

I knew she could talk. I knew she could hear. It was conversation about her ugly, old, beat-up, yellow Mini-Cooper (which she babies beyond belief) that earned her the nickname. Granted, I'd never heard her talk to anyone in recognition of a person's humanity, nor have I ever seen her smile.

"And that, your honor, is why I killed her."

"Case dismissed!"

So I had made it my quest to confuse her into saying something to me before life took our paths on a new direction and our deep friendship faded into history. I had decided she must be a lawyer. Yeah, a lawyer.

I checked the mail on the way out of the building, which basically meant that I glanced to my left as I passed the mail room to see whether any white was peeking through the holes of the box that had my name.

> **Note to Self:** *Stop on the way back to pick up the mail.*

I pushed through the door and asked the guy at the front desk to turn on the taxi light. I was out the door and into a taxi. I gave the driver the address on Diversey Parkway. I sat back, set the box on the seat, and the bunny on the box. I thought about Mini-Cooper girl one last time, wishing I could have handed her the box and walked away.

It dawned on me that I might as well imagine Ms. Mini-Cooper taking the box. History said that had I actually given the box to the sour-faced young'un—though I might have elicited an accidental thank you—I would never have seen the look when she lifted the lid to find a "Do-It-Yourself Kidnapping Kit," and instruction sheet inside.

Do-It-Yourself Kidnapping Kit
Materials: rope, gag, ransom note, fake newspaper with place to fill in the date (for proof of life)

Steps 1-6:
Tie yourself up.
Gag yourself.
Take your picture with the proof of life newspaper.
Send it in a ransom note to someone.
Make follow-up phone calls disguising your voice.
Collect the ransom without getting caught.

Step 7: *Tell me the story of how you did it.*

I was also certain that once she did, we would begin to have a functional conversation. It would be:

And that, your honor, is why I sued her.

Thus proving another axiom I live by:

Quite often the fantasy is far superior to the reality.

The story behind Evil Uncle Richard's present is short and quite sweet. He spent his off time as a director, watching and entertaining people as a host at a restaurant. It was the same restaurant that I frequented while I lived in a nearby hotel during my move back to the city. Our first conversation began with questions about the book I was reading and ended hours later with tales of our childhoods.

After a couple of years, we had reached that comfortable rut that friends do where we had stories of our own. One of our stories included the quip, "Oh, why don't you get yourself kidnapped so you have some new stories to tell?" I couldn't let him not go away to not join the army without that question in his repertoire.

Taking a check on the taxi, I knew this wasn't going to be a long ride. But all in all, I get bored easily. So I set my mind to getting interested in the details around me. I noticed that I'd become sensitive to big guys with dogs.

That sort of sensitivity is pretty typical human behavior. It happens to almost everyone. Teenagers in "love" start thinking that every person on the street looks like the object of their affection. People with a sick relative start noticing that every show on TV seems to be having an episode about someone in the hospital. It's not even a coincidence. It's more like the way it seems that every time you're away from work a really big problem happens. You think that the problem happened because you were away, but the same problems happen when you're there, they just seem bigger when you're not.

These days, there or away, big problems are hanging all over me.

In any case, knowing all of this has made me fairly immune to omens, coincidences, and things that happen when I'm away. But I still notice things. Patterns are too interesting to ignore and like I said, I get bored easily.

We were finally getting through the traffic on those last four blocks, which I think of as the Diversey drag—a part of this particular ride that I could walk backward on my hands and beat the traffic, despite the fact that I'm no acrobat.

Why do I always forget to tell the driver to take Broadway?

So, I put the bunny back in my pocket, put the box back on my lap and pulled out my wallet to pay for my ride.

As I looked up to check the meter something about two blocks ahead of the taxi caught my eye. A silhouette in the setting sun of a big guy—who might even be described as an oversized sixth grader—was crossing Diversey Parkway with a dog wearing a doggie raincoat.

A doggie raincoat. Who would put a doggie raincoat on a beautiful Weimaraner? Is someone under the impression the dog has not been wet before? A doggie raincoat on a Weimaraner? That could never be right. I must be having a synapse lapse.

I look again. It's worse. It's not only a doggie raincoat. It's a doggie raincoat—in "needy pink"!

The taxi stops. The driver says, "That's eight dollars, Miss. Miss?"

"Huh?"

"Eight dollars. On the meter."

"Um, uh, Could you? . . . Would you mind? Driving a little farther first?" I stammered, calculating the chance of catching up to the pair I was half sure I had seen.

"I'm sorry, Miss?" he asked politely. "Are you okay?"

"Ah no. Um, but thank you," I said stalling for time. Finally I resolved to end my ride there as originally planned. I reckoned that I must be seeing things—must be being oversensitive to men with dogs. I also figured that either way the chances of finding the big man and "needy pink" doggie raincoat were a bad bet. I came to the conclusion that no make-it-clear Weimaraner who had yet to share his name with Larry would be caught dead wearing a "needy pink" doggie raincoat.

I pulled a ten from my wallet, thanked the driver for the ride and for his patience, unfolded my legs from the taxi—which is no small feat when you have a box, a bunny, and size 11AAA feet—and was fully out in about three minutes. The man had earned his tip.

I stood on the curb looking west until the last of the sun had completely set. It was one of those rare sunsets juxtaposed against a lead gray sky. The whole world looked magical and more three-dimensional in some way.

I stood staring for what might have been fifteen or twenty minutes until Gunnar came out of his Flower Shop.

Petey's Posy Palace—don't ask.

He asked me if I was going into Richard's party or practicing to be the next Rolls-Royce hood ornament. I don't know if he noticed that I had no clever comeback.

"Yes, Gunnar, I'm heading to the party right now!" I cheered, coming to life with a vengeance. "Let's get this party started."

Gunnar and I walked in the door together and immediately heard Richard's booming baritone.

"My evil twin has arrived!" he called. "Get this Alice some wine."

The costume he wore was Spartacus. Okay, so I do believe in omens—when I think they're good ones. And this costume choice was a good one.

I think.

Chapter Five

Are We Going to Dance or Talk?

RICHARD HAD GONE TO FOLLOW his own order to get this Alice some wine. I set the box on a table and pulled off my coat. I hung my coat on the back of a chair and felt like a magician as I pulled a rabbit out of my pocket.

Rocky, watch me pull a rabbit out of my coat!

"We're not late, rabbit." I said, thinking this day had lasted longer than some weeks I could remember. "We're right on time." It was very good news to me that we hadn't beat Richard here. When that happens it's really sad.

The preparations were finished—another good omen.

Obviously, Dr. Dan and George, the two guys who were in charge of this bash, had done this kind of thing before.

Richard returned with my wine and a glass of Veuve Clicquot Champagne for himself. I accepted the glass with a curtsey to the floor.

Yes, Mom, I find every possible use for the 14 years of dance training you gave me.

Then we toasted our friendship and I toasted him a second time with a ritual best not shared in print.

I can say no animals were killed in the making of that toast.

"I hadn't even taken my coat off when you greeted me. How did you know I was Alice?" I said, with the kind of grin you save for those friends who fill your heart the second they fill your eyes.

"Well, sugar," he drawled. "You're such a silly putty combination of curious and sassy. It was the obvious choice. Besides the blue ribbon in the hair was a dead giveaway. Of course, had you been dressed in red, I would have said Freddy the Fire Truck, because you do talk like a runaway firehose let loose on the floor." Zing! Got me.

"Have I told you lately how much I love a man dressed in a dress who can still play a good game of verbal volleyball? Especially a guy with knees as cute as yours?"

"Careful, Miss Follow-that-rabbit-into-Wonderland," was

his retort. "This is my 'going away to *not* join the army' Roman army uniform. Do you like the sandals?"

"Why yes, Mr. Spartacus," I answered with the best Alice-respect-for-her-elders I could muster. "I find the sandals most fashionable and becoming. Though I do worry that they appear to be strangely lonely without your usual black socks, madras shorts, and push lawnmower." Touché (whew).

Richard flashed the evil twin look that said, "Ah, we're on our game tonight." Knowing that he was arming for a response I cleverly distracted him by setting down my glass next to the box on the table beside me. He spied the box.

The box itself was nothing special. It was a medium-size corrugated shipping box, the kind you get from a direct mail apparel merchant such as Lands' End, when you order something like four pairs of pants in size six with a 36 inseam. (I knew this because that's how I came to be in possession of this particular box.) It was the gift wrap that made the box quite so attention-getting.

The wrapping paper that covered the box had been designed by the seven-year-old down the hall on a rainy day sometime during the summer. He had complained of having nothing to do. I had handed him a roll of ugly wrapping paper and asked him to make it beautiful for me. I showed him how he could use wet crepe paper I had (from my "Arts and Crafts Director for a Summer Camp" past life) to make lightyears of improvements on the wrapping paper's design. The new design was quite colorful in a very childlike way.

I added visual attraction by weaving a string of Christmas lights through the bow.

When I set down my glass to distract Richard, I also flicked a small switch on a battery pack. So it was no surprise that the box caught his attention. Actually, it probably would have caught his attention from across the lake through a dense fog—still, it had accomplished what I had hoped; the subject was changed. Score two points for Alice.

I saved Richard the obvious questions by ceremoniously handing him the box and saying, "Yes, it's for you, and yes, you should open it now. Then it's your choice whether you wish to share it, display it, or hide it away from folks who wouldn't understand. Although inviting such folks to this party would be evidence of poor planning to the highest degree."

Once the box was opened, Richard laughed out loud. He said he wasn't quite sure how he was going to complete steps 2–6 *after* he had carefully tied himself up. He suggested that he might have to find another use for the kit. I told him I had faith he would figure it out.

Richard also offered a profuse thank you and made a promise to return the favor in spades. (I'm still a bit paranoid when I think just what that could mean.)

"Now, dearie, you haven't made comment one on the renovations I've made," Richard said in a bit of a snit. I looked around to see that all that was left of the original restaurant were the deep raspberry walls, a kitsch-lighted painting of gondolas, and the beautiful copper bar with its library lamps. Yet even that had been extended and modified to make it more attractive and comfortable. The copper was covered with red rose petals from Gunnar's flower shop. Light from the bar lamps on the rose petals reflected a soft pink back into the room.

But the rest of the room was as if from a slightly skewed seventies fairy tale. Where once there had been a banquet room, now was a dance floor, smooth as glass and perfect as water. Where once there had been a kitchen, now was a pizza and salad station—open and airy, accented with a faux skylight, as if it were in a friend's suburban basement. Yet the three looked perfect together, as if Audrey Hepburn had been consulted in designing them. Along the walls were comfortable couches with tables set as you might find them in the living room of that very same suburban friend.

"Hello, as I was saying . . . " Richard said to get my attention back. "My going away present to myself was to finish buying this place and to decorate it just for parties with my friends."

This was the perfect end to Richard's Chicago story—He had slowly lent enough money to the spoiled brat, Chef Jeff, the last owner of the place, to actually buy it out from under his nose. Even Chef Jeff's mother had approved the deal. This turn of events on the neighborhood bully would have been enough to make even Mini-Cooper girl smile, if only she knew how.

I was still laughing at Richard's coup, when two guys joined us. Their names were Pat and Riley. Riley had come as the Cowardly Lion. Pat had come as Mark Twain.

I asked, "Hey Pat, why'd you come as a writer instead of a character?"

It's not that Pat didn't know what was expected—come as a character was plain enough. It's more that Pat liked to futz with the rules when he could.

"I didn't. Well actually, I did both," Pat replied. Riley, who had come up behind Pat, began singing "If I Only Had the Nerve."

Not to be thrown, Pat politely waited. When Riley had finished the first verse, he asked Riley's permission before he went on.

"Now, where was I?" Pat retraced, playing it out for what it was worth. "Ah yes, the author-character dilemma. Mark Twain's real name was Samuel L. Clemens, right?" Pat pointed out.

"Yes. That's true, but—" I started to say.

"So," Pat interrupted, "if you think about it, Mark Twain could be considered a character, a character that Mr. Sam Clemens played."

"I don't know. That seems to be reaching a bit," I said.

"I understand your concern," Pat said. "I'd find my argument weak too. Don't take my word for it. Who am I to put forth such a premise?" And just as quickly as they had joined us Pat and Riley walked off singing the rest of the Cowardly Lion song.

I knew there was a reason I liked this crowd.

I looked at the rabbit I was holding and said, "See, I told you there was nothing to worry about. I'm never bored in this crowd."

As if on cue, in walked the Flintstones. Fred, Wilma, and . . . Bamm-Bamm? Not just Bamm-Bamm, but Bamm-Bamm in a baseball cap. Joellyn, a.k.a. Wilma, was a woman who owned far more character costumes than any grown-up should admit to having.

About that time the music started and the crowd began to grow faster than I could keep track of. Finally I saw our hosts. Dr. Dan had come as that 1950s Golden Book character Dr. Dan the Band-Aid Man, even though he hadn't been born when the book came out. And George had come as Curious George, though when they walked by he was asking Dr. Dan how to ease some sort of itch the costume was causing.

Looking around, I saw Mr. and Mrs. Franken Berry, elegantly dressed in their signature pink, sharing a drink with Katniss and Peeta from *The Hunger Games*. Two or three characters from *Lord of the Rings* sat talking near the pizza bar. Charlemagne was deep in conversation with Holly Golightly, while her date, Crocodile Dundee, was interviewing Sam Spade.

I had lost my wine glass almost as soon as I got it, but I was more interested in dancing anyway. I didn't feel like dancing alone and I knew the rabbit would spend the time looking at his watch were I able to talk him onto the dance floor. So I needed to find a partner.

It wasn't supposed to be this way. As soon as planning for this party started I had asked Craig to come with me. Craig is the guy you take with you when you go to dance clubs because he's so fabulous at dancing. He and I had even planned a special dance in Richard's honor but a recent mandate from Benny saying I wasn't allowed to socialize with colleagues outside of work meant Craig couldn't come. Craig was truly disappointed to be missing the party.

Finding a guy to dance with would be a challenge.

I headed off in the direction I had last seen Riley and Pat. I found them over by the DJ booth. Riley was talking music with the DJ. Pat was talking books with Charlemagne.

The DJ put on "(I've Had) The Time of My Life" by Bill Medley and Jennifer Warnes from the movie *Dirty Dancing*—great song to dance to, if you can find someone who knows how to dance.

In desperation, I just gave up and said, "I feel like dancing. Does anyone want to dance?"

A deep voice behind me said, "Yes, ma'am, I'd be honored."

I turned around and stood face to face, actually eyes to nose with a 6'2" Lone Ranger, who seemed uncannily familiar. And what do I say?

"You're no Patrick Swayze."

To which he replied, "And you're no Jennifer Grey. So, Alice, are we going to dance or talk?"

Chapter Six

A Complete Bio on the Lone Ranger

DANCE? WHO WAS THIS masked man? He called me Alice. Why hadn't I seen him at the party before this? Why was he asking me to dance? Something wasn't right.

My mind was racing with pictures of a guy and a lowercase 'd' dog interrupting my morning run. Thoughts of the Lone Ranger, who earlier that day had sent me into my head on a pony on a boat, and a silhouette in the sunset with a dog in a "needy pink" raincoat. My body was busy discovering the full meaning of the word *stunned*.

Somewhere around reaching 5'10" I had given up liking surprises. I had finally figured out that

> *grown-up surprises usually weren't much fun,*
> *and at the very least needed preparing for. I*
> *know that's pretty late to figure out such things.*
> *I'm a bit of a late bloomer about a lot of things.*
> *My friend Nancy says, "Sometimes you are so*
> *fast, and sometimes you are sooooo slow."*

So there I stood, just invited to dance by the Lone Ranger, frozen on the edge of the dance floor like the Alice in Wonderland version of Lot's wife. The feeling was the mathematical opposite of communing with the sky—my feet were stuck in psychological glue that was oozing over the floor. The walls were showing signs of closing in. (Weirdly, I was worried that I might be marking up Richard's perfect new dance floor.) Even my hair follicles were finding out what it meant to feel self-conscious. At least, they wouldn't be giving away secrets this time.

I must have been clutching the white rabbit for protection, because I felt the masked man gently remove my hands, one finger at a time, from the poor bunny's neck. As Tonto's friend walked over to the DJ's table to set the stuffed bunny aside, I felt a raging blush of embarrassment that started in the toes of my 17th century Alice shoes and rushed up the back of me to reach the blue satin ribbon at the top of my hair.

My mind was having a little trouble processing and this was not a good time to defrag my brain. My mental processor was locked and still flashing on that damn "needy pink" doggie raincoat—and the coincidence of my Lone Ranger morning. Then, like an automatic mental reboot, an "Aha!" moment occurred. I felt the palm of my hand hitting my forehead and with it came the biggest question of all.

Could this costumed cowboy even dance?

I could be walking out there with the biggest klutz on the planet! This could be the longest dance of my life. Who cares who he is? Let's get practical.

Could he dance? I was soon to find out. He'd asked me to dance to the most popular song from the most popular dance movie of all time—*Dirty Dancing*. Did I want to do dirty dancing with this guy?

Back from delivering the bunny to the DJ, the Lone Ranger took my hand and led me out to the dance floor. Apparently, he had asked the DJ to re-start the song, possibly a man-to-man plea on behalf of his bashful dance partner—that would be me—to give her a chance to get up her nerve.

The music began. We locked eyes—well, as much as you can when you're eyes to nose and one guy's wearing a Lone Ranger mask. I fell back on my dance training, letting the Lone Ranger lead and my feet just follow. We moved back. We moved forward. We did that cha-cha and I swished my skirt. Then we did the merengue. We did the dip and jiggle. He spun me out and pulled me in. We did the slide down the arm thing and the turnaround thing too. And through it all never broke eye contact. He could dance. So could I. Better yet. We could dance together like we were meant to.

Watch the movie, we did it all and then we made up some new ones. If you know the movie and you're wondering if we did the lift—you bet we did. Sometimes, life really does imitate movies. We did the lift again. Then the whole room started dancing.

It's a little eerie to think back on it—Spartacus, Mr. and Mrs. Franken Berry, Charlemagne, the Cowardly Lion, Mark Twain,

Dr. Dan, Curious George, Holly Golightly, Katniss, Peeta, Crocodile Dundee, Sam Spade, the bunch from *Lord of the Rings* and the rest all dirty dancing. I don't know how many times the DJ let that track play. It seemed like we were dancing through time and everyone was bumping and grinding.

The dance was romantic. The room was electric. The mood was magnetic. The crowd was eccentric. The effect was mesmerizing. I had made it to Wonderland.

It was a roomful of Wonderland.

We lost all sense of time and all self-consciousness. We became what we were doing.

When the music was over, so went Wonderland. Like a little kid, I suddenly felt separation anxiety—the hole left by the missing stuffed bunny.

"Thank you for the dance, ma'am," said the Lone Ranger, escorting me off the dance floor. Preoccupied, I looked back for globs of glue where I had been stuck to the floor before the dance. I'm sure I showed visible relief at seeing none.

"I think I need my rabbit," I said.

"I'd be honored to retrieve your pet, ma'am," said the masked stranger. Did I hear a hint of an accent in there?

"Thank you, and uh, could you quit with the ma'am stuff?" I asked. "I'm beginning to feel like I've landed in an episode of an old TV western."

"Yes, Miss Alice, I'll do that," The LR answered. I heard an accent, I was sure of it.

"Oh, get the rabbit and quit talking." I all but ordered. I had always liked men with accents, but this one was getting on my nerves. I needed him gone so that I could get some information.

At his first step, I was off to get Richard. I needed to find out who this guy was.

"Richard, there you are." I said as I got to the copper bar. Without missing a beat, I reached across the red rose petals, and poured myself a new glass of Ronco Cucco. "I need your help. In 25 words or less, I want the complete bio on the Lone Ranger."

"Well, let's see, the legend says that six Texas Rangers chasing outlaws rode into an ambush, and all but one were killed. That last guy living called himself the Lone Ranger. He donned a mask, found a brave Native friend named Tonto, mounted a horse named Silver, and loaded his gun with silver bullets to protect the people from outlaws."

I took a quick sip of my wine and complimented his memory, "Good job. Nice bio—concise and factual. But that was 60 words and that's not the Lone Ranger I need-to-know about. I'm talking about the guy who's coming this way with my white rabbit in his hands."

"Him? The guy that you were dancing with?" Richard asked. "I thought he came with you."

I was afraid he was going to say that.

"Here's your white rabbit, Miss Alice," said the Lone Ranger, brushing off the stuffed bunny. "I have looked him over, and he seems to be in good working order."

"Thank you, Mr. Ranger," I said in my Alice in Wonderland voice. "I'm sure Mr. Rabbit appreciates your kind care."

"You are welcome, Miss Alice. It was my pleasure to help," the masked man replied.

"Um, Mr. Ranger, would you mind answering a couple of questions?" I asked sweetly.

"I would be happy to, Miss Alice," he answered.

"What's your name and where are you from?"

"I am Des. Des Gardner."

I knew it! Nothing North American about that name . . . or that accent.

"You're not from around here. Are you?"

Sounds like a line, but it's what I was thinking. No, it's what I was feeling—blunt and to the point. I wanted answers.

"No, mate, I'm from Sydney but I live in LA," Des explained.

Mate—guess that's the difference between the Lone Ranger and Des. Well, at least, he'd dropped the Miss Alice and the ma'am stuff.

My better self realized that I should breathe a little and be more gracious. I took a sip of wine before I continued. I asked Des if he would like something to drink. He said he thought a beer would be nice. So we headed toward the copper bar. On our way, Pat and Riley walked up.

"Hey, you two, that was a dance," Riley gave us a high paw.

"Heck," Pat agreed. "I haven't danced like that since work yesterday."

I thanked them for their encouragement and pretended that I was enthralled with Des. They got their drinks and went on their way.

"Des Gardner," I repeated. "So are you?"

"Am I what?"

"You say you're a Gardner, but are you a gardener?"

"Well, not really. But we've got some grass at the ranch," he smiled.

"No garden with bark mulch?"

"Sorry?"

"No garden with bark mulch . . . where one might work when one wants to think about not thinking?"

I watched his face for a glimmer of recognition. I was beginning to get suspicious that the Lone Ranger here just might know a certain lowercase 'd' dog.

"Who has time to spend time thinking about not thinking?"

I couldn't tell if he was serious or playing with me, but I had to keep going.

"Not even when you're thinking about not thinking while you're inside the colors of the sky?" I continued.

I was hoping to catch him off guard with my quick response.

I felt pretty clever until he said . . .

"So explain to me how this works. How does someone think about thinking about not thinking? And how does that someone do all that in the colors of the sky?"

"Oh. My mistake. For a second there, you reminded me of someone I know . . . er . . . well, sort of know," I blurted. "You're so smart. And it's obvious by the way you dance that you've been around the block."

I was recovering as best I could. Clearly this was not Larry.

"Been around the planet. Always enjoy the trip," Des offered, bringing the conversation back with a smile. "But you're the expert on Wonderland, Alice."

Score one for the cowboy, reminding me who I was.

After a second he paused. Then he asked, "Do you need an airplane?"

"Do I what?"

"Do you . . . need . . . an airplane?" he repeated slowly, as if English was not my first language.

"Not at the moment, thank you, but if you have one . . . I can save it for later," I replied at full speed. "World peace would be nice too." I added with a curtsey.

Then it dawned on me. He was referring to *thinking inside the colors of the sky. Did I need an airplane to be thinking inside the colors of the sky?*

"Oh. Uh . . . no."

At that, he just looked at me . . . and smiled . . . and waited . . . patiently . . . with an annoying expression that could only be described as fascination.

I felt everything self-conscious about me kick in.

I tried to block it. I tried to ignore it. I tried to lose myself in my glass of wine. I even tried thinking about thinking about not thinking.

"Okay, okay," I whispered "I surrender."

I took a deep breath and said, "Why did you come to Richard's party?"

"Who is Richard?" he asked. "I was told this party was for you."

Chapter Seven

And There I Was

"YOU THOUGHT THE PARTY was for me?" I asked incredulously. "Well, then the question is even more important. Why did you come to a party you thought was for me? We've never met. . . . Have we?"

"No, Alice. We haven't met. And it's a valid question. I'm happy to tell you the story of why I came. But first," Des said with a smile, "I need to get another great American beer." I made sure he had that beer before he finished the sentence.

I picked up my wine as he placed his hat and mask on the bar. The Lone Ranger was transformed into a real guy named Des. It felt better to see his brown eyes.

"I'm an actor. I'm here for a movie," he started.

I checked my radar for blips of insincerity. None.

"Which movie?"

He told me.

I knew the movie. Des's story still rang true. Just last week, a friend at work had gone on and on about watching the film crew down on LaSalle Street.

The movie was the second in a series, set in a dystopian Chicago of the future, a place and time where divergent thinkers are seen as threats to the existing social order.

Considering what was happening at work, I found these movies particularly compelling. Enough people seemed to be uncomfortable with my thinking lately. I knew what it was like to be surrounded by people who saw me as a threat.

"I heard about your movie," I said, bringing myself back to the conversation. "My friend, Craig, really enjoyed watching the film crew last weekend."

"Yes, I know he did. I'm the one who invited him to the shoot. Craig is my friend too," Des announced with a huge grin. "In fact, it was his idea that I should come to the party."

"What? Who? You know Craig?" My mind was spinning fast, and my words could hardly keep up.

"Yes, we're good friends," Des explained. "Craig's condo is my home away from home whenever I come to Chicago. I like to spend as much time with him as I can when I'm here. And I thought he'd get a kick out of seeing us work on the second movie, since he'd watched us work on a good part of the first."

"Wow," I breathed out while I considered this new information. "He's really your good friend too. I almost always hear the things that people aren't saying. When Craig talked about the filming, I'd figured out that he had watched for a while or he wouldn't have been able to tell us so much about it. He'd even mentioned that a visiting friend was with him. But I thought you were simply watching with him. . . . He never hinted that you were an actor in the film."

"Yes, Craig's always been good about protecting me like that," Des said with another huge grin displaying their friendship. "We've been friends since we met in college at USC. He lived right down the hall from me. For a while after, we even shared a place on the ocean in Seal Beach. But he moved back to Illinois for his career, and I stayed in LA for mine."

"I guess your loss was my gain. I can see why you became such good friends. You're smart and witty like Craig is. Craig's a great guy and he does protect people he cares about. I don't know how I'd get through work each day without him. Surely I'd be considered even more divergent in our dystopian workplace."

We both laughed at my oblique reference to his movie.

"So," I continued, "I feel caught up on the backstory. Now I could guess, but I'd really like to know how did you end up at this party?"

Des gave yet another huge grin and said, "It's a little like a movie plot. Craig and I talked about it at that same shoot last weekend. We were sitting under a tree, watching the action. We'd been talking about the film for hours. Finally I asked him if we could talk about his work for a while."

"Craig explained that publishing can be as dangerous as

acting, and even more bizarre," Des went on. "He described the guy who runs the place where you work as an extreme crisis manager who has no real moral code."

"He said that?" I asked intrigued, engaged, and maybe a little bit nervous.

"Well, maybe not in those exact words, but that's what I gathered," Des admitted. "When he got to the part that you were asked to uninvite him to a party, I couldn't get my head around it," he continued. "Why would your boss do that— tell you that Craig couldn't go to the party with you?"

I had trouble getting my head around it too. So my answer skewed to hyperbole. "Because he's afraid that Craig and I might be friends? . . . Because he believes that his worldview and supreme intellect allow him rights not granted to any other human? . . . Or perhaps because he's a crisis-inventing, tantrum-throwing, selfish child who really has nothing resembling a moral code? . . . Still, you just have to love him, don't cha?"

I stopped talking. My heart rate increased. My blood sugar level dropped. What was I doing? I hadn't understood the depth of my feelings. I was saying things. Even worse, I wasn't just saying those things. I was saying those things at a party to someone I barely know who knows someone I work with and knows that someone really well.

I felt as if the entire room had gone quiet, waiting to hear what else I might say.

> *Whenever I think the world revolves around me,*
> *the universe flies wildly out of balance.*

Most people haven't thought about it enough to know that so much of what we feel is determined by the point of view we choose. It's almost impossible to avoid feeling negative when we view a situation from our own individual point of view. When we do that, our assessment of that situation becomes not only self-centered but also often selfish. It's just so much easier when we look at where we stand to be aware of what's lacking or missing. And that sense of deprivation only fuels more selfish thinking.

"Oh my gosh!" I stumbled, attempting to adjust back to the positive. "I was joking. It's not really that bad. After all, I'm still working there." The hollow sound of my words hung in the air.

"No worries," Des said, lending me his calm and positive state of mind. "After all, I think you have to be at least that . . . um . . . self-directed . . . to get a job in the film industry." We laughed. And I did feel calmer.

"I guess we might not have met had my boss not made that 'uninvite Craig' mandate," I smiled back.

"This could be the start of the most amazing friendship," Des added, and he raised his beer in salute.

I touched my glass to his bottle and said, "Here's to Benny's mandate and the most intriguing outcome of anything any boss has ever requested of me."

Seeing what we have requires more energy and thinking.

Where we stand has no quality of positive or negative, for me or against me. It's our point of view that adds that filter to our feelings about where we are.

Emotions congeal uncomfortably when we want the world to see our point of view. Even our bodies can feel that. Emotions expand and dissipate comfortably when we choose to understand the world's point of view. We can feel our bodies aspire, actually breathe toward, a new sense of our own relevance. We connect with our value to ourselves and our value to the world.

With that toast and that new thought of how Benny's mandate had sparked a positive outcome, everything fell back into place. Two continents connected and we continued our conversation.

"So you still haven't told me," I said enjoying this new positive feeling. "Why did you come to Richard's party?"

Des ordered more drinks for us and settled into his story. "So Craig and I sat under a tree talking and he told me about how he'd been invited to a party by a friend at work. He explained to me that you two had a fabulous working relationship, that you enjoyed each other's company, and that occasionally you got a chance to not just work together but also to dance."

"That sounds about right," I interjected. "Not many folks know that Craig's a fabulous dancer, but I take advantage of it when I can." I smiled with affection for Craig.

"He says the same about you," Des replied. "Anyway, Craig went on and on about how you had been looking forward to dancing at the party. He was disappointed to find out he couldn't come, but I think he was mostly disappointed for you."

"Yeah, I was disappointed to find out my dance partner wouldn't be here," I said. "I wanted Craig to know that I disagreed with Benny's order to uninvite him."

"Anyway," Des went on, "Craig and I got to talking about who was a better dancer—Craig or me—and that discussion somehow became him saying that I should go in his place."

"What? Wait a second," I interrupted, "Craig decided that you should come in his place?" Craig hadn't said anything to me about sending a replacement. He had a whole week. Why didn't he say something?

The positive glow started to dim. I didn't like what I was hearing. "Craig decided you should come in his place? Is that what he said?" I tried to keep my cool.

"Actually, this time those are his words. He said I should go to your party in his place. When I said wasn't sure, he said that if I made certain that you had a good time, there'd be dinner and drinks at the top of the Hancock in it for me. He was focused on you getting a chance to dance and having a good time. I guess I just assumed the party was for you."

"Craig's not my keeper. He's not even my boyfriend. He doesn't get to decide things like that," I declared, feeling confused that Craig would send someone I didn't know to keep tabs on my evening. I would never do that to Craig.

"Please understand, Des, on all levels I'm really glad to meet you, but I'm really not okay with the reason you came. What else did he tell you?"

Des continued, "He said it was a character party. I would know you because you would be the six-foot Alice in Wonderland. Craig had planned to come as the Lone Ranger. By the time we got back to his place, Craig went straight to find his Lone Ranger duds and brought them to me. He made a comment that, in the hat and the mask, we even look alike. For him that sealed it. I should be the surrogate Craig. I would be your dance partner and you would have a good time."

I was speechless. First I saw bathroom signs that said "For a good time call. . . . " Then I thought of how sweet it was that someone cared. That immediately was followed by an eerie feeling that people were talking about me, and that Craig was out there somewhere watching me. The last thing I needed was another guy who had decided it was his job to keep track of me. I must have been concerned because I realized that I was holding the white rabbit by his left ear and bouncing his head off the side of my right leg.

This kind of thing was not consistent with the actions of my friends. My lifelong friends wouldn't even know about this party until they read this book—unless, of course, one of them happened to call or visit sometime around the event, and we found ourselves in need of a topic of conversation.

"A good time!" I erupted. "Well, I'm not sure I'm up for a good time." I blushed, thinking what Des might have misconstrued from the offer of dinner and drinks at the Hancock.

"Oh no," Des reassured me. "Craig was clear that I was to
see that you had a good time at the party, nothing more. He
said you don't like parties and I might find you sitting off in a
corner by yourself. He made it clear that in such case, I was to
take your hand and say 'Nobody puts Baby in a corner.'"

> *"Nobody puts Baby in a corner" was a cult
> reference to Jennifer Grey's character, Baby, in*
> Dirty Dancing. *She is about to perform on stage
> with Patrick Swayze, but her father tells her to
> sit down. (No favorite daughter of his is going to
> dance with a dirty dude like Patrick Swayze.)*
>
> *Good daughter that she is, Baby ends up backed
> into a corner at a table with a white table cloth,
> sitting with her parents like a six-year-old at
> a wedding reception. But Patrick Swayze in his
> black leather jacket and blue jeans—already
> wrongly accused of theft by the father—walks
> up, delivers the line—"Nobody puts Baby in a
> corner." Swayze takes Grey to dance to the same
> song that the Lone Ranger and I had danced to
> earlier that night.*

Nobody puts Baby in a corner? This was no coincidence. This was
premeditation. How could Craig do this? He knows I don't like
surprises, much less anything that smacks of a setup. What
was going on? I looked over at the DJ. The DJ who was there
before had gone. A new guy was spinning disks. Sitting in a
corner had begun to look very appealing to me.

I felt deeply uncomfortable now with this Lone Ranger,
co-conspirator friend of Craig's. Suddenly the situation felt

both dangerous and creepy. I had already said too much about my boss, and if Craig had lost his loyalty . . . if he had no problem with Benny's mandate . . . I needed to find out why he had sent Des in his place without telling me.

I walked Des over to meet Richard and introduced them. I also got Des another of his favorite American beers.

"This is the real guest of honor, Des," I said, "He's leaving to direct opera in Germany." They started talking operas and then movies, old and new. The conversation shifted to the techniques of great directors.

I had hoped the introduction would allow me to disappear for a while to sort my feelings. But before I could slip away, Dr. Dan called Richard over to say good night to some early departing guests. So I was left once again with the Lone Ranger.

I cut to the chase. Well, I gathered what grace I could and told Des that he had fulfilled his obligation gallantly, with honor and style. I thanked him again for the unforgettable dance, and I reminded him that he was free to stay to enjoy the party or to return to Craig's place. I needed him to know it was clear we were not a couple.

With a deep bow and his characteristic huge grin, Des chose the latter.

I wished him well in his movie—I think he was playing a faction leader—and his career. He invited me to have lunch on the set the following week. I said I'd try to make it, but I'd have to think about it. This surrogate Craig experience had been just too weird. I couldn't imagine having the same kind of fun talking as Des and I had enjoyed earlier, and if we tried, it would probably turn out quite awkward.

I was walking to the copper bar when my phone vibrated. I had a message.

Where I had it stashed was pretty clever—I'll just say that the darn bunny was more than an accessory. I have no time for a purse. I already told you I gave up that "I Think I'll Act Like a Girl This Year" life in about two hours.

I went outside to see who called.

I hit my voice mail. It was a message from Craig. "I hope you enjoyed my party surprise."

I was not happy. I was so not happy. I was furious.

I had not been that furious since Lucas had asked an FBI friend to follow me for eight days—for my protection—without telling me. I won't elaborate, because it would take about 23 chapters to tell the tale. The point is that after two decades he's still hearing about it. When I want to, I can still stir up what could pass for temper over it.

I walked back inside. I went behind the copper bar. I reached into the cooler. I took out an open bottle of Ronco Cucco. I smiled at Curious George. I took my emergency reserve wine glass with the passport wine charm from the mirrored shelf behind the bar.

I walked from behind the bar. I stopped by Richard next to the DJ table. He saw the passport wine charm on my glass and knew—this was serious. I told him that I was going to get some fresh air and asked him please not to forget about me. I also wrote a note to that effect and handed the note to the DJ. Bottle and glass in hand, bunny in pocket, fury on my mind, I walked out the back door.

Pure fury is actually a pleasant feeling. So often anger is mixed with other emotions. You know, anger mixed with insecurity, or anger mixed with fear. But point-blank, seeing-red, pure, you-are-so-wrong fury is a rare and fine emotion—one to be savored, preferably alone with a glass of wine under a clear night sky. It's also motivating, which was particularly helpful on this particular night. Because in order to get to the night sky with my glass of wine, I had to do something a tad out of character. Under other circumstances I might have called it brave.

Before me was an outdoor fire escape. I was about to climb it. I was about to climb it in my 17th century shoes, Alice in Wonderland duds, with bottle and glass in hand, and bunny in pocket. Which, to many people would not be a problem, but ironically, for a 6-foot-tall person, 6-foot-tall is about as tall as I like to get.

Still, I had a goal. I desperately wanted to be two stories up. I would climb. I climbed trying not to think about the getting back down part. I did not think about the times in grade school I hid to avoid fire drills that involved outdoor fire escapes. I practiced thinking about thinking about not thinking.

Eventually I was there. "There." I guessed if Larry's dog could be 'the dog,' I could call this place 'There.' There was worth the climb. Most people didn't know There was even there. There was a courtyard of sorts. Really There was an open concrete slab surrounded by four buildings. It was as if the buildings had declared the area between them a "no building zone."

Off to one side were condensers for the restaurant, hotel,

and stores around and below. Curiously, in the center of this concrete space was a living room set—a long sofa, a love seat, two stuffed armchairs, and a small coffee table. All were covered in a white and pastel flowered print. All sat on a large square of red carpet. A terracotta pot held a fake fern at one corner.

There was one of the happiest, most peculiar, and delightful juxtaposing of objects I could imagine.

I had often wondered about how There had come to be. But I figured that the fantasy was probably better than the reality. I had convinced myself that I didn't want to know. I knew about There, because I had spied it from the window in my hotel room when I stayed next door.

At that moment There was right where I wanted to be.

And There I was.

I sat on the long couch—which was miraculously dry, despite the forecast of rain. I poured myself a glass of wine, gazed at the passport wine charm, and leaned back to take in the sky. Time to clear my mind.

The fury was gone. I listened as the sky played the music of creation. I saw everything good in the world. I closed my eyes and wore the peace. Not thinking, just being. Finally God is in His heaven; angels are everywhere; and all of the people are at their own party—not mine.

I felt almost perfect. My eyes crawled into Orion's belt. I was thinking of all of the people who had seen it before me and all of the places I'd seen it before. Everything I knew and everything anyone had known seemed connected. I felt totally welcome on this planet. An incredible sense of belonging made me feel able to fly—a feeling I used to know . . . I tried to recall this feeling, but it was just out of reach. The space, the sky, the sense of being precious in someone's eyes was tangible and real.

I wondered.

I wandered.

I wandered through my wonder.

I wondered at my wandering.

How would it be if everyone felt this way . . .

. . . all of the time?

I stretched out on the couch, shoes and all. I closed my eyes again. I half-waited to hear my mother's voice telling me to take my feet off the furniture. But the voice I heard was not my mother's.

"I figured I'd find you here," said six-foot-two Larry sitting at the foot of the couch, as his lowercase dog jumped on the love seat. "Mind if we join you?"

Damn, just when I had everything sorted out, here comes the guy with the dog again.

Chapter Eight

The Sleep of the Innocent

"WAIT A MINUTE. You can't just do that." I sat up so quickly the passport charm rattled loudly against my wine glass. I set the glass down to steady my hand and still my thoughts. "You can't just do any of this."

"Do what? Do any of what?" Larry asked and a pair of caramel eyes echoed the question without a trace of guile. "Check in to see whether you enjoyed the party?" The innocence in that statement was aggravating.

"Check in to see whether I enjoyed the party? Seriously?" I said aloud.

Was this guy for real?

Actually *that* was a good question. *WAS this guy for real?*

I had met him this morning when I was running in my mind.
I had been sitting under the majestic oak tree thinking about
not thinking inside the colors of the sky, when this guy and
his dog invaded my mind uninvited. That was strange enough.
But this time they weren't on my mind, they were sitting right
in front of me. . . .

As far as I knew I was the only one who had seen them. But I'd
known them for less than 24 hours. How did they know to find
me up here? Richard was the only other person who knew this
place existed . . .

Was I imagining them? I *must* be. The idea that they would
find me or follow me here was too much for me.

Maybe this big guy and his dog were just a phantom, some
product of my imagination, a Fig Newton of my insinuation, a
fortune cookie of my intoxication. Had I fallen through some
rabbit hole into a rare state of Karma-skew?

Maybe I *had* met this guy before and I just didn't remember.
Maybe *not.*

I picked up my wine glass and in a thought I was at the small
bit of wall where you could look down at the city neighborhood
below. It was a busy shopping area where three streets come
together in a single star-like intersection. Plenty to look at or
ignore, depending on your frame of mind. I was choosing the
Lamaze method of thinking: focusing on one object and controlling my breathing to move all other ideas out of my mind.

A story occurred.

❖   ❖   ❖

We were standing in the kitchen, the room where all serious family dialogue seemed to take place. Was that because it had four escape routes, each leading to a completely different part of the house?

"You don't know anything about this guy," my mother was saying. "He appears out of nowhere and you just trust whatever he says?"

"Mom, he's a nice guy."

"You, who wear your feelings on your sleeve, would know a nice guy from a con-man? How can you be sure he's a nice guy? You've hardly spent any time with him at all. You have too many feelings out there for the world to see. He could be just reading you like a book. I swear one day the world is going to eat you alive."

As my eyes welled up with feeling, I had to admit that she was right. I did have too many feelings. I'd always had too many feelings and they'd always shown up at the most inconvenient times—like right then when I was trying to make a point. I knew, intuitively knew, from those too many feelings knew, that he was a nice guy. And it had proved true. He was an exceptionally nice guy.

She never gave credence to the fact that he turned out to be a nice guy or that some things in life you just know. Even though she was more intuitive than I was then. It was as if, for her, that conversation had never happened. But in so many ways she let me know that my feelings were my greatest weakness.

❖   ❖   ❖

I wasn't sure which nice guy—Craig or Larry—had triggered that story. Because neither one seemed particularly nice at this moment, even though I was pretty sure they both had it in them.

I took a sip of wine and I lingered at that small bit of wall, looking down at people I didn't know. Some who knew each other. Some who did not. Some who had probably just met. Perhaps even a first date or two. Most of them were walking down the street, crossing the street, waiting to cross the street, or trying to flag a taxi. They could be anyone. Larry and the dog could have been among them, and they would have gone unnoticed. They would be only two more warm bodies in that picture of moving humanity. But they weren't down there, they were up here, which was There.

When I went running in my mind this morning, I was happy being me, myself, and I. I mean, I was doing okay. Except for the debacle at work, my life was going. . . . Well, it was going by, but I guess it wasn't really happening.

Now, not even 24 hours later, I had two problems: this guy and his dog who spoke as if they knew me better than most anyone, and my friend Craig, who really did know me better than most anyone. Both were trying to take care of me. Both were watching out for me to make sure that I didn't shoot myself or something.

Why was I feeling so aggravated?

I picked up my wine glass and in another thought I was back on the sofa. I took comfort in that dealing with Craig felt like working with a known, and saw relief in that dealing with Larry and the dog felt like dealing with a known unknown. Both led me to return to the place I had left.

I have a high sense of fairness but, real or imagined, this guy and his dog seemed to think they could just show up in my head uninvited whenever, wherever, and however they pleased, asking questions and looking at me. I looked right back at them.

"As I was saying, you two can't come and go in and out of my head as you please. At least, that is what I was trying to say."

"You don't want us to care if you're happy?"

I looked at the soft-spoken man and said, "Grrrrrrrrr."

Then I looked the sweet-faced dog in the eye and said, "and you, be quiet."

That done, I picked up my glass, moved my legs onto the couch next to me, lifted my hair to fall over the armrest, rested my head where my hair had just been, and turned to make friends with the sky. My audience could look all they wanted. My hair follicles and all of my secrets didn't care. I was going to commune with the sky, and they could do whatever it is they do. (Perhaps the Alice outfit had taken control of my mind.)

I was determined to forget they were there.

And it worked.

For a while.

Until Larry started snoring.

Then it got worse.

The dog started snoring too.

They were snoring in harmony. . . .

. . . And that was distracting me from my aggravation.

I didn't know snoring could be musical. But two totally different species were making music in their sleep. Blissful sleep, I might add. At least it appeared to be. They slept the sleep of the blameless and their sleeping made music.

As affronted as I was that they could forget my agitation so quickly, I was mesmerized. It was wonderful. No, it was awe-inspiring. It was a night-like score befitting a daydream.

Soon my head filled with the sounds of a symphony. People took their places. Einstein was conducting. The passionate voice, Lisbeth Scott, took the stage. An audience of formal wear went silent in anticipation. I had the best seat in the house on the sofa under the stars.

Scott began to sing the amazing Glenn Frey and Don Henley song, "Desperado," and at the start of the second verse, Peter Gabriel stepped out from the curtain to make it a duet. Their voices wove together in a tale of loneliness and unrequited love. But the song had never made me feel lonely. It always sent my thoughts traveling back to through time to my earliest childhood memories. Even before my brain could understand it, I knew about love.

⊰⊱ ⊰⊱ ⊰⊱

I was in my childhood bedroom. I was really short. I couldn't have been more than three. It was time for my afternoon nap.

My dad came home from work. He worked incredible hours. I wanted to stay up to be with him, but my mom said, "No, it's naptime." Like any small child, I didn't like to take naps. So my dad said he would lay down with me until I fell asleep.

In minutes he was snoring, but I was wide awake. I kept ever so still for ever so long so as not to wake him. I tried to breathe exactly the same as he did—in . . . out . . . in . . . very slowly—so as not to disturb him.

He needed sleep and he was my dad. He loved me and I loved him. That's how love works—you take care of each other. Even a three-year-old knows that.

⇥ ⇥ ⇥

The uncanny symphony of snoring brought me back to the concrete living room. I was again under the sky. Larry and the dog still were enjoying their symphonic sleep. After this little side trip in my head, all I could see was the child and the puppy they once were.

They slept as if they had not a care in the world. Those cares that they didn't have obviously did include me.

What was I supposed to do?

Wake them to tell them that they look sweet or that I don't mind that they're sleeping?

What could I do, but let them sleep?

I went back to the stars, back to thinking of the places that I'd seen those stars and the people who had seen those same stars before me. Somewhere out there in the night sky, I finally realized that I needn't let this big kid and his oversized pooch scare me. God was still in His heaven; angels were still everywhere; and I still had my place in the universe.

I swear at the very second I had that thought, the harmonic sleepers awoke with two loud discordant yawns.

I started laughing.

I wasn't laughing at the yawn, but at the way my eyes had proclaimed its truth before my mind could make sense of it. I saw the words, *Rug-Pulling Roller Coaster Twins*, in neon over their heads. The words perfectly described my experience of the crimes this man and his canine accomplice had committed. Continuously, they pulled the rug out from under my worldview. They kept the ground shifting under me. Every time I found my feet, Laurel and Hardy here showed up to knock me over again, always leaving me a little more confused by what they said.

"You seem much happier now," Larry observed, shattering my giggly mood to dust.

"Why do guys do that? You'd never do that to another guy," I said as I sat up.

"Do what? I simply observed that you are feeling better."

"Not that! I am feeling better. But I'm talking about what you did," and saying that, I placed both feet on the edge of the table. "I was upset, and you two just went to sleep."

"It looked like you were so aggravated that you had stopped talking to us and decided to look at the sky for a while."

"I had."

"What's a guy supposed to do?" Larry asked with sincerity. "Soldiers and spies have a motto about preparing for war: Sleep while you can, because you never know when the chance to sleep will come again."

"What a great way to show that you value our relationship: think of my aggravation as opportunity to get some shuteye!"

"You could think of it as ducking for cover," Larry offered.

"I let you know that I was aggravated by your unceasing intrusions," I whispered. "And . . . without the tiniest syllable of apology, YOU lean back and fall asleep! No one would mistake that for owning the fact that you had caused my aggravation! Or that you cared that I was aggravated!"

"Let's get some food," Larry suggested in his most charming voice. The dog wisely declined to participate.

"You and your dog, and now even Craig, keep insinuating yourselves into my life. You do it to make sure that I'm okay, but when I'm not okay, you try to escape by going to sleep. And when that doesn't work, you suggest we get something to eat? Priceless!" I stated simply, trying to look calm and relaxed.

The dog wasn't buying my instant replay of events, but I didn't care.

"What? I'm not sure I . . . we . . . know what that means. I simply thought that we all might feel better sharing our feelings while we break bread," Larry quietly explained. "Could we . . . ?" He hesitated. ". . . do that?"

"No."

"Oh, Alice."

And the way he said it, with such generosity, made me stop to take a breath. So I did.

After a moment Larry calmly asked, "Where does Craig fit in all of this?"

"Craig tried to take care of me too, and it felt even worse."

"What do you mean? What felt worse?"

"Let's see." I got up and began walking as if teaching a class.

"Remember this? Girl goes running when the sky is that blue-black that stops time, tricking just about everyone into thinking that morning is a long way off. And as she's letting her thoughts sit out in the colors of the sky, you interrupt her to find out if she's safe."

"Ohh," Larry moaned. Both Larry and the dog changed positions uncomfortably. "Well, we . . . "

"GRRRR . . . " I said, staring them back into their previous positions.

"Now, imagine this," I continued. "Girl asks first boy—who in this case would be Craig—to go to the donkey baseball game. For some wild reason, first boy isn't allowed to go. So first boy tells second boy—who in this case would be a friend of Craig's—to find said girl at the donkey baseball game. He tells him she'll be the one wearing a red rose."

I leaned forward to make my point. "First boy doesn't ask girl whether she wants to be with SOMEONE SHE DOESN'T EVEN

KNOW at the donkey baseball game. First boy DOESN'T EVEN CONSIDER that girl might have made other plans after first boy couldn't go."

I gave the dog a long look that said, "Stay out of this. It's not your conversation."

"But you didn't make other plans," Larry noted.

The dog just nodded, as if to say, "He's right, you know."

"Which brings me to my next point," I said circling his chair. "Craig PAID a guy to dance with me. He said there would be dinner and drinks in it for the guy. I don't know how Craig knew I would be Alice, but he did. Then he TOLD SOME STRANGER to dance with me."

I liked that one. It was an easy one, I'll admit, but the logic was there.

"You could look at it that way, I suppose," said Larry, all patience and light. "But let me ask you: under all of your aggravation about Craig not telling you that he had sent Des in his place, do you think what he did was mean, or intended to trick you?"

"No. Actually it was one of the most thoughtful things anyone has ever done for me," I admitted. I reached my hand down and the dog came over, so that I could scratch his head. Through that contact, I got in touch with my true feelings. "It just scared me. You know, . . . when I found out that Craig arranged this, but didn't tell me, I got scared. I had trouble trusting. But you're right. Craig's never done anything mean. He was making sure I had a good time."

"So rather than choosing fear, why not accept his gift in the spirit of generosity with which it was given?" He leaned back in the armchair and stretched his legs out to their full length.

"So, Larry, would you help me set aside some lingering questions?"

"Anything to help you, Alice."

"How did Craig know I would be dressed as Alice? Why the Lone Ranger?" I asked, sitting on the arm of the couch.

"Alice was an easy guess. Who else would you be? Every close friend of yours has heard the story of how *Alice in Wonderland* changed your life. In fact, I bet you told me you were going as Alice," he smiled, eyes closed with his hands behind his head. "The Lone Ranger was harder. Don't you think Craig knows that you're a fan of the old TV show, and that you like Lyle Lovett?"

The dog had started looking from Larry to me to Larry to me, as if shaking his head at both of us.

"How would *you* know those things?"

"You told me."

"I did not."

"Yes, you did. More than once." A person listening would think that he was being angelically patient with a small child or an incredibly forgetful relative.

Not wanting to get into a "did not—did too" argument with a

guy who is bigger than I am, and also just as sure of himself, I let that one go.

Which is not to say I acquiesced. Anyone—even people who have never heard of me—will tell you I don't usually acquiesce. I find it hard enough to think the word. Besides *acquiesce* sounds like something that a jellyfish would do right before it gives birth. . . . *The female jellyfish acquiesces and the young jellyfish are born swimming off and then back to their mother.*

"What about the line from *Dirty Dancing* that Craig told Des to say?" I challenged, leaning forward and forcing Larry to open his eyes.

"You were listening to the *Dirty Dancing* soundtrack this morning when you were running. It's reasonable that you would know that line when you heard it." Larry smiled right back into my eyes. His words were making sense, but they were hard to hold onto.

Ever had a conversation with a close friend in front of another person, where everything you said had another meaning—a second meaning that only you two friends knew? It felt like that's what was happening with Larry, except that I wasn't in on the secret. I couldn't quite grasp the real meaning. I just knew that Larry's answers were a little superficial. It was as if they fit too perfectly, made too much sense. I was missing something. I needed some key to this code.

"Why would Craig offer dinner at the Hancock to be sure I had a good time at a party he couldn't attend?" I slid down onto the couch.

"You already know."

"I do not."

"You do too."

"How do *you* know what I know?" I said, exasperated and tired of talking about it. "In fact, how do you know any of this?"

"Oh, Alice." Larry sighed again. He tilted his head and stared sadly skyward. I felt like a child who couldn't keep up with the big kids. The dog wisely laid his head down on his front paws.

"How could you not remember me? I've known you since you sorted your first box of eight crayons. That was long before the box of 64." Larry put his elbows back on his knees, laced his fingers together, and just stared at the concrete for a few minutes.

The dog barked his assent. I wondered what they were seeing.

My mind tried to take in what he had said, but it made no sense. I met this guy and his dog in my head this morning and then again here tonight. The time had come for me to find a new conversation.

"Everyone who knew me that long is long gone," I said, standing. "I need to go back to the party."

Whatever this man thought, however long he said he had known me, what he was saying was just not possible. He could not have known me that long without leaving a trace of a memory somewhere in my head. Every guy I had known had entire diatribes about my memory. The descriptors included *absolute*, *relentless*, and *pain in the butt*. The idea was pushing the realm of impossibility. I couldn't conceive of a world in which I would forget about, lose track of, or in any way let fall aside the existence of a person who had been part of my history, as this man kept telling me he had. I do not forget people.

"Do you ever think about why it is that you spend so much time thinking about not thinking?" Larry asked, looking up. "Or why it is you feel best when you're looking at the sky?"

I heard the questions. I decided to let them sit in the air.

Who knew? A well-thought question might enjoy sitting in the air as much as I do, given the chance.

I started gathering my things, but I couldn't help thinking about Larry's question about my thinking. I tried not to. I knew that thinking about why you have been thinking is much more work than thinking about thinking about not thinking. I grabbed the bunny off the table and put him back in my pocket.

I knew that it was especially dangerous to be thinking about why you have been thinking about not thinking when someone is watching you thinking. I poured my wine in the fake plant.

I realized I wasn't going to be able to get down from There because it's exponentially more dangerous to be thinking about where you are while you are thinking about why you have been thinking about not thinking when someone is watching you thinking. There. I stood There staring at nothing.

"Do you suppose that any other person would have heard those two particular people—Lisbeth Scott and Peter Gabriel—singing that particular song? *Desperado?* Or had

Albert Einstein as their guest conductor?" I heard him, but I didn't respond.

No points for those questions. He was just showing off. I had already done my wondering about those two questions. I couldn't bring myself to think the word *thinking* at that moment. I was barely fit for wondering.

I surrendered myself back to one of the armchairs and put my elbows on my knees. The Rug-Pulling Roller Coaster was moving again.

"You shouldn't be surprised that you don't remember me. In many ways, you hardly remember yourself. You hardly recognize your own name . . . there was even a boy who called you Sue, wasn't there?"

"Well, yeah, I didn't want to embarrass him."

⊰⊱ ⊰⊱ ⊰⊱

His name was Bill. He was a year ahead of me and really cute. I think I had a crush on him. Somehow he had decided my name was Sue and I couldn't bring myself to correct him. I'd rather be Sue than embarrass him.

So I arranged all kinds of scenarios in which friends would call me by name, hoping he would hear. But the scenarios never worked. I was always Sue to Bill.

One day, May Miller, Diana Drummond and I were in May's VW. We saw Bill walking home. May pulled over to offer him a ride. Diana said she'd move to the backseat. Bill said, "No, that's okay, I'll sit in back with Sue." Diana said, "Sue? Sue?

There's no Sue in this car!" Both Bill and I burned red and dissolved into thin air. I think he decided to walk. I don't remember talking with him or even seeing him ever again.

⊰⊱ ⊰⊱ ⊰⊱

"In the end, you didn't save anyone."

"The pain was unbearable. But you know, I didn't mind him calling me Sue. I like the names people make for me. It lets me meet new parts of myself."

"Or it lets you give new parts of yourself away."

"A rose by any other name . . . " I had him on that one.

The dog had heard enough and said so with a large woof.

"But don't you think you should have a name for yourself? A moniker tells people who you are. Your brothers, cousins, and friends all call you by different names, and you've yet to choose one from the bunch for yourself. I wonder why?"

"Maybe I have a favorite name. But like the dog, I just haven't shared it with you," I smiled.

"Maybe you don't and you're just trying to change the subject," he smiled back.

"Look at these blue eyes," I said with a smile and a Dennis Quaid glint in *my* eyes. "Would they ever lie to you?"

"No, they never lie. I know that." He said this in all seriousness. "They would tell the truth and make it *sound* like a lie."

I couldn't help myself. I had to respond. He was trying to pin me down, and I was trying to get out. Time to go back to the party for sure this time.

"I need to go back to the party. Uppercase 'L'—you—and lowercase 'd'—he—keep pushing into my discomfort zone. I know you want me to remember you. I'm sorry I don't. I would like to be generous and help you with your quest. But you want me to explore this name thing with you, and I don't want to do that. Again, you're insinuating yourself into my life."

"That's a good, thinking woman's rationale," Larry observed.

I swear, if a dog could applaud by just looking, this dog was. I couldn't tell whether the applause was intended for Larry or for me.

"Now, you're making this about *me*," I said. "This isn't about *me*. It's about *you*, prying into my life."

"Sorry," Larry said, "I was just voicing what I see. You do that too, don't you—for your friends?"

I felt the dog adjust the score—Larry two, me nought.

"Not fair. I might help a friend when his thinking is stuck," I said, "but I won't throw out 656 questions while a discerning dog is keeping score."

At that moment I was replaying every conversation I'd ever had with every friend I had ever known. And at the same time, I was wondering what my name really was. Then, out of the blue I remembered that I didn't have a favorite color until I was 31. On the flower scale of people, I felt like the world's latest bloomer.

"I'm going to call you Angela."

"What?"

"Angela, it means 'angelic'."

"What?"

"Angelic."

"Yeah, right. I know what it means. That's me—angelic."

"Doesn't mean you can't aspire to be. With your brave heart and your vulnerability, I bet you'd make a darn good angel, if you put your mind to it," he said.

"I thought that being an angel was an assignment. You know, uh . . . *You three over there, you're angels. You six are humans. Sorry, Mike, you're an ass* . . . that kind of thing."

"Still worth aspiring to. Don't you think?"

The dog, obviously feeling sorry for me, came over and put his head through my arms. It was an easy pull of my elbows off my knees into a hug around his neck. Immediately I felt alive—the emotional bank account refilled back to balance.

I closed my eyes, leaving Larry behind. His voice faded into the background.

⊰⊱ ⊰⊱ ⊰⊱

I saw big hands, the hands of my father. One was on the steering wheel of the car. The other was holding my much smaller hand. The sun was shining brightly down through the windshield onto my face.

"Who put the sun in the sky, daddy?" said a four-year-old me with too much light in my blue eyes.

"My mother, who is a very wise woman, told me God did." His voice wrapped me in unconditional love.

"Why did God put it there?" I asked, curious even then.

"So that the sun could rise and set on your precious head," he answered. "So you are always warm and always have light to find your way wherever you want to go." And because my dad told me, I knew it was true.

"Do you like the sun, Baby Doll?" my daddy asked.

"I like you, daddy," I heard myself say.

❊·❊ ❊·❊ ❊·❊

I was still scratching the dog as I watched the memory fade.

I don't know how I happened to fall asleep, but I did.

Chapter Nine

It's a Doozy!

A THICK CLOUD COVER had fallen over the outdoor space. I moved through it, approaching the fire escape to head back down. I was uncomfortable with unenclosed heights on any day or night for that matter. But this gummy cloud had made me even more apprehensive.

Clearly, it didn't matter how much I protested their intrusions into my thoughts. Real or not real, this pair had no need for permission slips.

Larry interrupted my thoughts and my way toward the fire escape by saying, "Why not go through that window and take the stairs?"

My voice tried to communicate a sense of calm as I said, "What a great idea. Thank you." But the rest of my body seemed to shout its agreement. An overwhelming sense of relief flooded through my every pore.

Larry held the window, while I ducked through. Then he handed me the white rabbit, which must have fallen out of my pocket. I think the dog stayed back by the outdoor living room.

I headed down the stairs back to the party. The hotel stairway seemed to move as if it were made of water. The rabbit and I moved ever so slowly as we made our way down. I told the rabbit that I was worried that we would be too late. And in that same second, we were back at the party.

The bunny and I pushed our way into the party room. We caught glimpses of almost everyone—Trinity, Holly, Croc, the *Lord of the Rings* group, Dr. Dan, Curious George, and others— almost everyone, except Richard. I called out his name, but he appeared before I made a sound.

What happened next felt like a movie plot.

"Hey, Spartacus, what time is your flight?" I asked Richard. "You know I wouldn't ask, but the rabbit worries about being late."

Richard reached into his Spartacus uniform to retrieve a printout of his itinerary. He handed it to me.

A brief look at his flight time and, in a split second, Alice in Wonderland was transformed into Alice the Operations Manager. Even my long apron and dress were changed into a sweater and jeans.

Most of my friends are "operations managers"—people who make sure the planes, trains, and any shared event happens on time and in the manner it should. I'm not naturally drawn to this job. Personally, if it's not part of my work life, I don't care what we do or when we do it. In my view, it's the people, not the place, that make the good times roll. So it's good to have friends who are, or we'd just sit around saying things like "What'da you wanna do?" "I dunno. What'da *you* wanna do?"

Operations managers are a lot like navigators. It's really best to have them around one at a time. When you're in the room with an operations manager, you should turn your natural management skills to low or you'll end up un-managing what's just been managed. Or worse, discussing philosophies of management while nothing gets managed.

So I'm all for letting my operations manager friends manage away. They tell me when and where to show up. I'm there, raring to go, and dressed for the event. But the part about making the plans and decisions—I find that most people care more about what happens than I do. I get to make enough decisions of that sort at work. Maybe too many these days.

So there we were. I (now Alice the Operations Manager) was looking at Richard (dressed as Spartacus) and his friends (dressed as a variety of characters) who had been partying for several hours.

I said something like, "Okay, Richard, your flight departs in five hours. They want you at the airport at least two hours before an international flight. Do you have your bags and your passport here?"

Richard finished the story he was telling Curious George and turned back to me to say he did.

"Great. It's gonna take about 30 minutes to get to the airport tonight," I figured out loud. "So you get changed and we'll get this place cleaned up. What time is the DJ supposed to finish?" But when I looked over to the dance floor, that part of the room seemed to be gone.

Dr. Dan slurred something about a two o'clock license and I thought it was good that he wasn't on call this early Sunday morning.

"It's 2:00 now, and our soon-to-be-departed Richard needs to be our dearly departed soon," I pointed out, living up to my manager role. "I'll call a limo. Richard, does 2:30 work for you? That gives you time to check out the International Lounge before you have to sit on the plane for hours."

Maybe, with practice, I too could be an operations manager. I could see myself rearranging pallets and skids around a massive warehouse.

"No limo! Spartacus will ride in a friend's chariot. Dan and George will take me," Richard announced.

As I said, I'd already taken an assessment of Dan and George and they weren't going anywhere. Both moved as if they were trying to walk across an icy road.

"Richard, none of you are driving anywhere tonight. Don't you want to change out of your costume and do those things that men do before they get on long flights?" I asked.

He laughed, saying, "Alice, the army paid handsomely for a first class ticket so that I would direct their opera. Let's give them a grand surprise. I want them to see me in Roman soldier uniform when I arrive."

I didn't fight. I told Richard I'd be back in less than 10

minutes. And the next thing I knew, I was on the rooftop in the outdoor living room again.

Lucky for me (and Richard), big ' L' and lowercase 'd' were still there, still absorbed in their silent conversation.

"Uh, sorry to interrupt." I had a feeling they probably knew what I wanted already.

"Yes, we do," was all Larry said. It was as if these two had a GPS chip implanted in my brain. They seemed to know exactly when, where, and what I would do next.

"Well, what I was wondering is, um, whether you would have a car, and could do me a favor?"

"We're happy to help," said Larry, obviously sensing my urgency. Perhaps he noticed that I hadn't stopped even to glance at the sky.

I explained Richard's need for a safe ride.

What was I thinking? Why would I suppose that these two would be safe? As my mother had pointed out, I hardly knew this guy. Well at least, I *did* know my way home from O'Hare.

Larry said that the dog and he were delighted to be of service, and that he would have his driver bring the car around.

And just like that, we were back at the restaurant. We helped the party come to its natural conclusion. We wished the last guests a safe way home. We sent Dr. Dan to take care of Curious George. His itch seemed to need immediate attention as well.

When the driver arrived, he reached for Richard's bags, which were right by the door.

"These?" he asked.

"Those and the three of these," Larry said pointing to the dog, Richard, and me.

Richard and I linked arms to walk out to the curb, prepared for what was bound to be a Medusa mess of legs tangled together in any car Larry might own. I had him figured for a PT Cruiser. Anything but a Mini-Cooper suited me fine.

But there at the curb was a trip back in time. It was a midnight blue miracle of a car, screaming for James Cagney to be leaning against it. A fairy godmother would have had to provide such a beautiful carriage for commoners like us in this day and age.

"Whoa! It's a Doozy! How'd you pull this off, Larry?" I stared in disbelief.

"You had a lot to do with it," he said. "And then, I simply asked my driver to bring it over."

What? I suppose in my wildest dreams I might have conjured up such a ride, but . . . we didn't have time to follow that comment down some secret Larry rabbit hole.

"Yes, but this is . . . " I said. I had trouble forming words while I marveled at the elegant machine from the past. It was an almost ten-foot-long, sleek body to die for, with six wire wheels, chrome-rimmed bug eyes, and foot-wide running boards. Everywhere you looked you could see yourself in the shine. This was one well-cared-for car. No bug dared die on this windshield.

"Is this car street-certified? Where does he keep it?" I asked the driver softly, as Larry and Richard packed the car. I swear I saw Spartacus drool just a little.

"Yes, it's certified, as are his Packard and his Daimler. But Larry prefers to walk when he can and so does the dog. He keeps the cars at a vintage dealership downtown."

The driver opened the passenger doors. The off-white leather interior was stunning and buttery smooth. The accoutrements were gold. A ride to the airport seemed too short a distance to take it all in.

As we drove off, I felt more like Cinderella on her way to the Oscars than Alice in Wonderland, riding in this movie star machine. I took the white rabbit out of my pocket so that he could share the experience.

The luxury of it all made us beautiful. The driver looked dashing. Spartacus looked manly. (You could tell he preferred this ride to a chariot.) Larry and the dog? They looked like Larry and the dog wherever they were. That was part of their charm.

That's how we—Larry, the dog, the driver, Spartacus, and Alice in Wonderland—came to be in a 1932 Model J Dual Cowl Duesenberg Touring Car heading toward O'Hare Airport on the Kennedy Expressway out of Chicago in the wee hours of a Sunday morning. We took our time, as Harry Chapin once said, "It's got to be the going, not the getting there that's good."

The going was good. It fit the three criteria for an event that showed we were truly alive—a noteworthy experience; a great story to tell; and the picture was priceless. In this case, even Sotheby's might agree on the priceless part.

The nature of our transportation and the style of our fashion garnered attention from those at the airport at that hour we arrived. That, and a set of important looking badges and a gun (with appropriate paperwork) that Larry flashed, first got the police to allow us to leave the car in their care and then got security to let Richard and the rest of our motley entourage through the VIP check door with minimal hassle.

We found ourselves in the International Visitors Flagship Club, but no famous names were standing around waiting to see us. I found a bottle of Veuve Clicquot in my hand, and made a champagne salute to Richard's departure. Next was a thank you toast to Larry for the ride in his handsome automobile and the perks that came with it. Somehow, Richard was getting a sendoff he would never forget.

The whole trip was a grown-up surprise that you didn't have to prepare for. I'd take a surprise like this any day.

Before we left, I took the blue satin ribbon from my hair, signed the back with our names and the date, and placed it around Richard's neck. This soldier had a lady's favor going into battle. Then I watched my evil-twin Spartacus walk through the gate to his airplane.

Larry talked with his driver as we backtracked through the airport to the car. The dog and I shared a companionable silence, walking at the same pace, not trying to fill the nonverbal space.

It seemed strange that no one stopped our group as we walked the concourse. But then, who would stop Alice in Wonderland for walking a dog in the airport? Either way, Larry's arsenal of badges surely would settle the matter. Actually, the dog's caramel eyes would diffuse any situation long before Larry reached for a badge.

This was one powerful dog at my side. It was like walking through the airport with Morgan Freeman (or Bruce Springsteen). Those who recognized him wouldn't think to interrupt or fawn. People kept their distance, clearing a wide path as if the dog were enchanted.

The concourse turned into a long tunnel. But instead of a light at the end, somewhere an old movie projector was showing "old movies," except they weren't old. I saw images of Richard's flight across the Atlantic. The flight attendants were talking to him, bringing him food and drink, and laughing at his stories. They seemed to like him as Spartacus. I saw images of his reception at the Frankfurt airport as he marched (or wobbled) out of customs. The American soldiers who collected him saluted. I guess that says it all.

When the home movies went to black, we were in the car. The driver and the dog sat in the front. Larry and I shared the back. I sat myself by the door and looked out at the sky.

Then a voice in my head broadcast aloud, *Here we are again, a mere 24 hours later, at that time when the sky tricks people into thinking they have more time than they really do.*

Before I could even think to quiet it, everything changed.

Chapter Ten

Shine On Harvest Moon

I LEANED AGAINST THE DOOR, staring up at the night sky. I had always liked the cool glass feel of a car window against my face. Suddenly I was in a 1966 Pontiac with my dad.

❧ ❧ ❧

Dad and I were on our way home. It was a road we had traveled often. This road connected his mother's home to our house. Trips to Grandma's with my dad were speckled across my life like so many snowflakes speckled across a night sky.

I knew this trip in many variations. I'd been taking it since before the Interstate made the trip shorter, since before our car had air conditioning, since the days before seat belts when I could ride in the car on my grandmother's lap.

My grandmother was all I could wish—she was tall, majestic, and magically intriguing. Everything about her was a trip back in time and across the ocean. Her front yard was rows of apple trees. Her kitchen had a water pump where you would expect a faucet. Barrels on her back porch caught rainwater for washing. She had no need for indoor plumbing.

I had no Italian. She had no English. Yet through gestures and the tiny Italian vocabulary she gave me, we enjoyed hours in each other's company. Funny faces I made for her were rewarded with genuine laughter.

It wasn't hard to love her. I felt love when my dad and his mother talked in Italian near the apricot tree in her garden. I saw it in the smiles in their eyes. I heard it when they said "buona serra." Of course, I loved her.

But this trip was different. We weren't on our way home from Grandma's house. We were on our way home from my grandmother's hospital room. I was looking out the window at the sky, when my dad said, "That's the last time you will see your grandmother alive." I looked at my dad and saw a tear running down his cheek. She was my daddy's mother. We both loved her.

❧ ❧ ❧

I looked over to see my dad, but I was back in the car with Larry. So much had happened since this guy and his dog had shown up yesterday.

All of the scenery switching was overwhelming. I just wanted to be. I just wanted to be thinking about thinking about not thinking. I needed to go running soon. My head needed defragging desperately.

I turned back to the window. If I kept my eyes heavenward, the view was calming. The glass still felt cool against my face. The seat was a comfort. But I realized that the past few hours had left me drained and feeling lonely. I tried to play some music in my head, but a million thoughts like fireflies were dancing to some unfamiliar tune—it was the opposite of having a song stuck in my head, but equally as irritating.

I found the sky again.

The sky isn't the same when seen from a moving car—unless it's a convertible. Inside a car, the car is between me and the open sky. The relationship is interrupted. Like when someone talks to a prisoner through a glass partition, it's not the same as being there. But it's still the sky, not a roomful of people.

I was peopled-out. The vision of fireflies in my head turned into people flying around me—people on the street, people from work, people from the party dirty dancing in costume—all flying around me. Then a fiery billboard lit up with these words my mother used to say about hanging around with the wrong people.

All the fireflies in the world cannot light your way out of hell.

And I started to giggle about the way I had gone from fireflies to hell on earth.

Lucky for me, right about then the Doozy reached my building.

I thanked Larry, his driver, and the dog for everything they had done. All three jumped out to open doors and say good-bye. I felt like Alice in Princessland as I floated out of the fabulous carriage. Even the stars were with me, because at that very moment, Mini-Cooper girl came out the front door to see us getting out of the 1932 Model J Dual Cowl Duesenberg Touring Car. What a perfect ending to a day.

I waved good-bye to my friends, and found myself in my living room. Then I heard a "yip" and looked up to investigate where it might have come from.

My ceiling dissolved into the night sky.

"Huh! What?" That was when I awoke. Awake? AWAKE? I had been sleeping? I found myself stretched out on the couch in the outdoor living room.

When I looked around Larry and his lowercase 'd' dog were sitting there with these Cheshire cat grins. (Yes, a dog with a cat grin. It *can* happen. I saw it.) They had knowing grins that seemed to say they had been there—at the party, in the car, at the airport, on the way back—playing themselves in the movie I had just dreamed.

I tried to make sense of the story I had experienced in my sleep. "Larry, do you have a car?"

"Yes, I have three."

"Is one a Doozy?" I asked hoping with all hope that he would say something like, *well, one is an old clown car, a VW Beetle once used in a circus.* But no, he said the last thing I wanted to hear.

"As a matter of fact, I do have a Doozy. It's a 1932 Model J Dual Cowl Duesenberg Touring Car, midnight blue with an ivory leather interior. Anywhere you look at it you can see yourself in its shine."

What was going on? It was disconcerting enough when *he* knew things about *me*. How did I dream up a car that he really owned?

Listening to my thoughts again, Larry replied, "Of course you would know. It was your idea."

"What do you mean, it was *my* idea?"

"From the beginning, you said I would own three movie star cars. And I do," Larry answered simply, smiling with pride.

"I said that you would have not one, but three, movie star cars? And you know this how?"

"Because I know you. It's my job."

He was talking in code again. How could knowing me be his job? He wasn't detail oriented or creepy enough to be a bodyguard or someone charged to write my dossier. Besides, Lynch had already started a dossier on me in college. Wait! Did this friend of a no-name canine know my theater friend from college? That was impossible. Right?

I tried to find a comfortable place in the sky to rest my thoughts. But I kept thinking of the connection between people and problems, causing that fiery billboard light up with my mother's words again.

All the fireflies in the world cannot light your way out of hell.

"You don't seem to like people much, do you?" Larry said softly. Again, he knew what I was thinking. While he was at it, he was interrupting my attempts to find a comfortable place to rest my thoughts. I decided to quit trying to fight it, at least for the moment.

I turned my eyes to his with sincerity. "Actually, I like them a lot. Too much, probably. Though I do prefer them in smaller doses. One or two at a time is optimal," I answered. "In larger groups, they're harder to understand. Groupthink kicks in and they wear me out."

I turned my head back to the sky. The stars, the one or two that you might catch in the city light, had long since disappeared, but sunrise was still a long wait away. This was my time. I wasn't going to miss it for conversation—not on a day that had been filled with too many words already.

But then I spoke anyway.

"Watching the sky makes me feel whole. Being with people often makes me feel like I have something missing. Watching the night sky makes me feel I belong to the universe," I added as an afterthought, still focused on somewhere comfortable out in the sky.

We sat in silence for a short while. For a moment I might have fallen asleep again because I found my feet pulled up under my skirt. I wasn't quite sure how they got there. Larry had laid his jacket over me. That was sweet.

"Was there ever a time when you were afraid of the dark?" Larry asked. I got the feeling that he already knew the answer. The question must have been more interesting than it seemed, because the dog's head appeared over the edge of the coffee table. Those caramel eyes were attentive and fixed on me, awaiting the answer.

"It took me a while before I got to be friends with the dark. I had no need for a night light. My bedroom always felt safe for thinking, imagining, and sleeping. But once the sun went down, going outside (or down into the basement) became a frightening proposition. Wild, winding stories would capture my imagination, holding my courage for ransom," I said.

"One recurring story was a bizarre kidnapping threat about getting snatched when I carried the trash out our back door to the bin about four feet away. First I would sing to distract myself, but then I worried that kidnappers would want a girl who could sing to sing for them. . . . So I would sing badly, until I conjured up kidnappers who wanted a bad singer— someone who would give them a reason to be mean. . . . Sometimes I would run to get there faster, but soon enough I thought of kidnappers looking for girls who could run. . . . So I would run with a limp. . . . The problem of thinking too much started early for me. I can only imagine what kidnappers would do to find a girl with that sort of a wild imagination."

"Quite an imagination still, as far as I can tell," Larry replied. "So how did you get past your fear of kidnappers to make friends with the night sky?"

"I took a walk with my dad and he personally introduced me to the sky," I said.

❄ ❄ ❄

When I was about half my size, maybe eight, I thought I was very worldly. My dad took me for a walk across our backyard out to see the river. It was fairly early on an October evening, probably near seven or eight o'clock. We were out to see the harvest moon. I was cold, but I wasn't about to show it.

"Look at that moon, Baby Doll," my dad said pointing out the light that made our way.

"It's so big, dad. It's so yellow. Look at the face of the man. He looks like you," I laughed.

"Yep, except he's a few years older, I think," my dad said. "The Man in the Moon is always there, you know, even when you can't see him. He's there."

We sat down together under the oak tree on the riverbank and sang a chorus of "Shine On Harvest Moon," laughing at ourselves after we did. We sat together watching the moon over the water without talking for the longest time. Until I broke the silence.

"I know how the moon got there, dad."

"You do?"

"Yep. You hung the moon, just for me."

※ ※ ※

"What is it about the sky that you like so much?"

"You mean, besides the lack of people asking me questions and the lack of dogs looking at me? That would have to be the sense of space, the closeness to God, the room to be me without anyone judging," I answered almost too quickly not to be revealing.

The dog agreed with a "yip." But I'm not sure whether he was agreeing with what I said or with the fact that I answered too quickly.

Now seemed like a really good time to go back to the party. Richard had to catch a plane and I had to stop revealing things.

Which also meant it was time to muster that brave heart that Larry had alluded to earlier—going down the fire escape was going to be harder in these 17th century shoes than coming up had been.

I giggled at the saying—*Be careful how you treat people on the way up, because you'll meet them again on the way down*—at least I was safe on that count. I had gotten here on my own. Ha!

Coming up I conquered the fire escape with fury. I needed motivation to help me conquer it going down. At one point, frustration with Larry would have made it easy. At another, fear could have carried me down. Now, I would try thoughts of my father and other words that start with "f." I was hoping they'd keep my mind busy as I navigated the climb down the perilous fire escape.

Those thoughts were conflicting with thoughts and images from my wild movie-plot dream as I headed toward the fire escape to return to the party.

An overwhelming feeling of déjà vu flooded through me, engulfing every cell. Would this count as my first attempt to return to the party? . . . or my second?

Then Larry said (again?), "Why not go through that window and take the stairs?"

Either way, the stairs were definitely a better idea.

Chapter Eleven

The Keys to a Friend

LARRY HELD THE WINDOW (again?), while I ducked under his arm and onto the stairs. Then he handed me the white rabbit, which had fallen out of my pocket, the bottle of wine, and my passport charm wine glass. The dog stood back by the living room waiting, as if he and Larry were going to have a pow-wow.

Fighting to overcome the tsunami of déjà vu, I began making my way back. The stairs were a secret passage through the hotel to the party. The hotel had been my home away from home for nearly seven months when I moved here.

A night security guard had shown me the secrets of the hotel. Markings on the brick walls near the freight elevator from the days when a famous Chicago gangster ran a speakeasy across the street. The markings were road signs to the underground passages. Lawbreakers could evade the cops and make a safe getaway in those passages.

The familiar sea foam carpet and light oak wainscot walls of the stairway felt like my safe getaway. My trip up the fire escape hadn't been the calming break from the party I'd hoped it would be. So I lingered on the stairs, taking my time, breathing in the safety of this secret space.

I was in no hurry to be among people again. When I reached the lobby, I still took my time. I waved a cheerful hello to the guys behind the front desk, Alfonse and Stephen, both of whom had treated me well. And I asked Armando how his quest to be a graphic designer was going.

Despite my dawdling, all too soon I was back at the party. I took a visual check. Things were calming down. The Franken Berrys and a group of others were gone. I didn't miss a chance to bid them farewell, because they were the "slip-out-when-no-one-is-looking" kind. The *Lord of the Rings* group had joined Trinity, Holly, and Croc in a deep conversation about life on other planets. I figured that in ten minutes or less one of the group would be voted most likely to find the answer.

As I walked by I heard Holly clearly saying, "I don't care what you think. I still believe in monsters. Terrestrial or extraterrestrial doesn't really matter. I'm always prepared that one might be somewhere around the next corner."

"That's my Holly," said Croc. "That's why she keeps me around. I'm her Mister Master Monster Manager."

The party was getting along fine without me.

I checked in with Richard.

"Hey, Spartacus, what time is your flight? I wouldn't ask, but the rabbit here likes things on time," I said, a little worried myself that Richard could be running late.

"Printout of itinerary in black bag behind the bar," Richard smiled, pointing to it and adding a "Would you mind, darling?"

"Be happy to, my love."

I retrieved the bag and returned it to its owner. Richard pulled out the printout, but spent an inordinate amount of time looking at it and his phone. Watching him look from one to the other I got an eerie premonition about whether Richard would get on the right plane at the right time.

I opened my heart and extended my hand. Richard placed the printout on my outstretched palm. I took the document, unfolded it, and set it on the hostess stand under the light.

I looked down at the flight arrangements. I closed my eyes to map out the sequence of events and the timeline needed to complete them in the right order.

My mind's eye flashed a glimpse of myself dressed as Alice the Operations Manager. Ack! I dismissed that image as quickly as it came. This was *no time* for *anyone's* version of Standard Operating Procedures. We needed to get this train on track (or plane in the air, if that metaphor suits you better).

I looked up and saw Spartacus and friends, who had been partying for hours. The way they were leaning and the bawdy tunes they were singing proved that driving did not belong on the menu of tonight's activities. At this point, I wasn't sure any of them could spell *airport*, let alone get to one safely.

"Well, it's time for things to start happening," I said, that sense of déjà vu rising.

"What's the hurry? My flight's not until almost 6:00. Why get things rolling so early?" Richard whined.

"It's already past 1:00. We still have to empty the room and clean up," I said, sounding like my mother.

Richard started walking people out. It took about 15 minutes to say the last good-bye and maybe another 30 for Richard, Dan, George, and me to clean up what little mess was left behind.

It's always good to invite friends in the hospitality business to your party. They make sure most of the cleaning up is done before they leave the party.

When we had finished, I watched Richard walk out with Dan and George. He helped them pour themselves into a taxi. I waited with his bags, recalling the memories and friendships that the now quiet room held. It was bittersweet to be standing in a testament to good times and great friends. Luckily, I retrieved my jovial mood before Richard returned.

"Success! Quite a sendoff, yes?"

"Ah yes," Richard said, looking like he was recalling memories and friendships as I had. He finally added, "The last of many such good times . . . Until I return!"

"Okay, Richard, everything's put away. It's 2:30 already," I said. "Do you have a ride to the airport?"

The sense of déjà vu swelled up again. Please say you've got it covered.

"Yes, I have transportation. Dan and George are giving me a ride."

No.

"No, they're *not!*" I exclaimed, with more passion than I expected. "You said good-bye to Dan and George. I heard you tell them not to worry. They said *bon voyage* to you. I saw them head home in a taxi. You stood at the curb, waving good-bye."

C'mon, evil twin of mine. Tell me you're just playing with me.

"Yes to all of that, Alice, my love," Richard said with clear sobriety. "Last week, I told Dan and George that we'd ride to the airport together. I'd even hoped that we would. But my years as a bartender/director have taught me about human nature. I knew it was unlikely that my two friends would be . . . [ahem] . . . *able* to drive me to the airport. So I arranged for a limo to the airport last Wednesday. It will be here at 2:45."

Whew! What a relief!

"Perfect, that gives us some time!" I smiled, knowing that it was this thoughtful Richard that I valued most. "So are you headed upstairs to transform from Spartacus into Richard again?"

"No," Richard said, smiling his mysterious Evil Uncle Richard smile. "I'd rather have this dance with you."

And that's how I came to be dancing with a Roman soldier in an empty restaurant when his singing was the only music that could be heard. When we stopped, he bowed deeply and led me to a place by the bar.

"Are you sure you don't want to change into something more

comfortable before you get on an international flight?" I asked, thinking of what I would need to do to get my head ready for an airplane full of people.

"No, I don't," he said calmly. "I look forward to seeing my army friends faces when they meet Spartacus in baggage claim—not to mention the looks from the flight attendants and the other passengers. My army friends have invested a healthy sum in a first-class fare. I'm guessing the airline is used to quirks—like a Spartacus or two—in the first-class cabin. And Spartacus can wear my coat to make sure that security stays calm."

"Are you sure your army buddies have your sense of humor?"

"Yes, I'm quite sure, Alice," Richard stated, taking on a professorial gait. "My army friends will enjoy the grand surprise to see me arrive in uniform. I told them I would. I just didn't say what kind of uniform," Richard laughed.

I knew which fights to fight and which fights to leave alone.

"I'm so going to miss your worldview," I said, my eyes trying not to swell.

Richard took my arm and escorted me to the door. He switched off the lights. He led me out the door and I waited while he locked it.

As we turned to walk toward the automatic door out to the street, he placed the keys in my hand. "Here you go, evil-twin girl, party or hide, as you will. I suspect you'll do more of one than the other." He winked. I held the keys and hugged Richard into my list of lifelong friends.

I felt lucky to be alive.

I looked at the keys in my hand in bewilderment. Feelings of surprise and gratitude were hard to hide. Feelings of loss and sadness were showing too. I loved Richard that much. I couldn't find words to express what I had going on inside.

I must have been looking at the keys for a while, because Richard came up behind me and whispered, "It's about time you figured it out, evil-twin girl. You can't get rid of me that easily. Now weren't you the one barking about the plane I had to catch?"

I would miss him dearly. I was already looking forward to the day when he would return. His brain, his humor, his generosity, all of who he is make the world a better place. It never crossed my mind he might feel the same about me.

Don't get me wrong. I knew we were friends.

> *The easiest way to tell if someone likes you is by how much you genuinely like that someone. If you very much enjoy someone's company, it's highly unlikely they don't enjoy yours. We tend to like people who like us. We think that they have really good taste. We think they're smart too.*

I held the keys so tightly it hurt my hand. Friendships rarely are returned as deeply as Richard's gesture had shown his friendship was. I seem to recognize those rare friendships only when someone makes it undeniable. I love my evil-twin. His gift meant even more than it was worth. I'd never forget how easily it was given.

Every now and then, an angel makes himself known by

doing something that says, "They don't know you like I do." Everyone—even the most misunderstood—has this happen.

Be sure not to ignore it when it happens to you.

I held those keys as we walked to his limo. I was still holding them after our final good-bye when I flagged a taxi going the other direction to take me home. I had them when I remembered and retrieved my mail. They were still in my hand when I got out the keys to my condo to let myself in (which is a bit of a feat).

Finally home, I set the mail, my keys, and Richard's keys on the desk.

Ready to end this rather long day, I went about unpinning the apron that was pinned on something on someone. Though I'm not one who likes to unpack or put things away, my fragmented brain found comfort in the basic work of folding the 11 yards of white fabric, lovely linen and rayon blend, lightweight, yet practical, which would be charming with any ensemble. I changed into a t-shirt, carefully hanging my perfectly blue dress and poet's blouse.

Some of that meticulous folding was to dismiss the fact that I was experiencing an unsettling transition—I had gone from being with many people I like to being with none at all. It was a swift and powerful loss.

When deep feelings accost me, I move to low-thought, high-visual accomplishments—in this case, meticulously folding 11 yards of fabric. Accomplishing a simple task and seeing that positive change helps me to reconcile my worldview.

Yet, some of that meticulous folding was transitional

procrastination . . . at the highest level. Smack dab in
the middle of that many-to-no people transition, I was
procrastinating to avoid an even more complex transition. I
was about to take a shower.

Taking a shower is an extreme transitional challenge.
Stated simply, it's a transition getting into the shower and a
transition getting out.

I made my way into the shower. It took forever, and much
puttering before I got to where water could reach me. I let the
water drench me, expand me, and release me. Stress washed
away, leaving a sense of wellbeing. Then I made my way out
of the shower. It took a second forever, and more puttering
before I reached dry land.

I surrounded myself with a huge terrycloth bathrobe and
savored my reward. For at least a split second, I was the
cleanest person in the universe.

I dried my hair, and checked the time. It was already well past
3 o'clock in the morning. The sky was still that backlit blue-
black that stops time, tricking me into thinking that morning
was a long way off. So I took my newly calm state to bed and
became one of those serious folks tucked in tightly. I was
glimpsing the clock with one opened eye, clutching frustrated
thoughts of why I couldn't sleep.

I made a valiant attempt to settle in for a short summer's nap.
Unfortunately, my brain was having none of it. The sun would
be rising soon. It was time to go running. I needed to sit in the
colors of a sunrise.

Back at my desk, I picked up the keys Richard had given me.
I held them in front of me, staring as if spying a fine crystal

Christmas ornament. After a while, I leaned back in my chair and closed my eyes.

"People can be grand, can't they?" Larry said, as if for no reason.

Again he interrupted my thinking and again I felt like I was in a conversation with two meanings. Still, I was determined not to care.

The dog barked softly, offering his own thoughts about Richard's gift.

My eyes fled the scene. I simply wasn't ready to share the space in my head. I looked for a mindless activity to lend me a sense of control and accomplishment.

The box of mail on my desk became undeniably attractive. Mail had been accumulating since work had started to go south. I'd ignored all but the most urgent of it with much success until now. Now I started going through it piece by piece. I stopped to read a note from Dianna about the house she and Clare bought and the home they are making.

> *Note to Self: Call Dianna next week, before you get sucked into another big project at work.*

I stuck a note on the Super Coupons envelope reminding me to ask them to remove me from their list. I read and tossed a notice from building management about fixing the garage doors. A few catalogues tried to entice me to buy things I didn't need. I put them under the Super Coupons also to ask them to remove me from their lists. Lastly I attended to the small batch of bills that hadn't gone paperless yet. One by one, I tossed the extraneous paper. Next I slipped each invoice under the flap of its return envelope. Then I laid them in a cascading pile in the order they were due.

This time I was meticulous mail sorting. Why? Was I overwhelmed with feeling? . . . procrastinating a transition? . . . or something else? My instinct said it was something else that kept me from putting on my headphones to go for a run.

I picked up the poem *Bother* that was still sitting on top of its folder on my desk. I was bothered enough to read it a few more times. Still bothered, I finally returned the poem to its folder and put the folder back into the file cabinet.

Why did I have this feeling of impending doom?

I reached across my desk to retrieve my first edition *Alice in Wonderland*. I took a moment to page through it again. This time, I found something. An envelope had been placed inside the back cover of this first edition.

I didn't remember placing anything in this book ever. Except yesterday before the party, it's been years since I've opened that book. Why didn't I notice this envelope when I got the book out?

The envelope was addressed to me at my parents' address. I hadn't lived there since college. It didn't have a return address. It didn't have a stamp. I didn't recognize the handwriting. I pulled out my letter opener with the star at the end. I opened it.

A drawing of a harvest moon over the giant oak tree in my childhood backyard fell open onto my desk. I picked it up and saw my dad and me sitting on the riverbank under the oak tree. The title read

Me, Daddy and the Man in the Moon.

The handwriting looked like a child's handwriting—not just any child's handwriting. Mine. I stared at that picture for a very long time.

Just hours ago, I had told Larry that story.

I didn't remember drawing it.

Chapter Twelve

Needy Pink Alert

I DON'T KNOW HOW LONG I stared at the drawing before I turned on my computer to find some serious running music. I needed to figure out how they pulled this one off, or at least make friends with the idea that I hid a drawing from my childhood in a first edition of *Alice in Wonderland.* I was baffled . . . bewildered . . . flustered.

Choosing music and choosing where to run when you're flustered is a logistical problem—a problem of the chicken-and-egg sort.

Do you find the music, then choose the route? Suppose you choose the music, and the route calls for something totally different?

OR do you choose the route, then find the music? Suppose you choose the route, and you don't have the right music?

Do you end up at iTunes spending hours and a lot of money downloading a new playlist, never getting to the run?

Seeing flustered as an emergency situation, I decided to let the music be my guide. I started scrolling through the thousands of tunes I own.

I needed music I could listen to and tune out simultaneously— if you can't do both, it's impossible to run through your mind. You end up just listening to music. You need to think deeply about the stories you find.

I was listening to REM, "She Just Wants to Be" and I thought, "Yeah, guys. That's it. This she just wants to be somewhere. And she's pretty sure that the somewhere is NOT HERE."

Good point.

On the thought that I wanted the farthest from here that is close to here, I decided to head to the Cloud Gate in Millennium Park.

The plan was set. The music was selected. The destination was decided. Time to don the appropriate running wear. Today's choice was the deep purple active wear with the white accent stripe. The color would play well under the chrome cloud that we Chicagoans call the "Bean." It would be fun to watch the stripe change shape in the reflection of the Bean.

The day's humidity screamed hat. This outfit called for the black ball cap with the single word *Perfect* in gold letters across the front. It had been a gift, but I hardly ever wore it.

When you're tall and blonde, you can't wear a baseball cap that says Perfect, without attracting disapproving looks.

Rather than ask about it (and finding out that it was a gift) people simply assume that you have it because you believe the word applies to you.

Cap was on. Shoes were on. I sat in my desk chair and leaned back. I pulled on my headphones and set out for the Cloud Gate.

I headed down Lake Shore Drive to the park, feeling the sun on my back. The movement felt great, especially the chance to weave in and out of the cityscape at my own pace. For a second, I thought about stopping at the Hancock bar on the way back for a cool one. Just as quickly I decided my refrigerator would do fine.

Deleting all of the traffic and the boring parts of the run— another perk of running my way—I got to the park in record time. I planted the oak from my childhood right where I wanted it. This time I also had imported part of the riverbank on which it usually stood. I moved my headphones to a branch of the oak tree, and on that small slope, I took up an observation of the people acting like monkeys as they watched themselves in Anish Kapoor's Cloud Gate, aka the "Bean."

Cloud Gate is shaped like a big silver jelly bean, which means it meets the most basic criteria of good design. It appeals to the adult (cloud) while appeasing the child (jelly bean). It's elegantly simple. It's made of seamless panels of highly polished stainless steel—that have the fascinating appearance of liquid mercury—forged together to make an elliptical shape that reflects both the park and the city skyline. The giant jelly bean is 66 feet long and 33 feet high. Walking through and around it resets a brain to do a double take on reality. In a way it's a metaphor on a life—on the outside, you see the universe reflected back at you; on the inside, you see yourself.

People swarmed in and around Cloud Gate, probably because the giant chrome cloud distorts them so. You can't help but get a new perspective seeing your reflection stretched and smashed. It's illuminating to watch how people behave when they do.

After a while, the people I watched became so much scenery. It was calming to be in the company of people without having to talk to them.

Ahh. To think and then to dream.

I wondered whether I would have been afraid of the Bean when I was a child. I was a fearful child. So the idea isn't entirely out of the question. But I did have a fascination for light and color and its smooth surface didn't seem threatening. So I figured I would have liked the Bean . . . provided that no one expected me to climb it.

A mere suggestion of height, and before I knew it, I was thinking about tall people again.

Tall boys get the first dates. Tall girls get told they look like models. Tall people make more money, get better job evaluations and quicker raises. Tall men who were short in high school earn like short men, but tall men who were tall in high school earn like tall men. When we're escaping the *Titanic*, we look to the tallest person in the lifeboat to save us. When a tall person enters a room, more people notice—a tall person takes up more space. A tall person is better protection against an enemy.

When you put people who are used to being tall around people who are even taller, something happens. The shorter tall people begin to act like children, as if that's the last time they remember being short. The point is even tall people act differently around taller people.

I walked over to the Bean and drifted through. I savored the feeling of stepping through liquid mercury, studying the distortions without being stuck. People around me were so engrossed in their own reflections I was invisible. I was in my element, invisible and engaged at the same time. Yet on the periphery I noticed someone I knew—needy Danielle. What was she doing in my head?

Most people I know have met Needy Danielle or her counterpart Needy Paul. They have either had one as a friend or, even worse, dated one. Most probably they haven't named what it is about their Needy Friend, but they recognize the description. Try it sometime. Supply this description and see what happens. Remember to change the names to protect the needy.

Needy Danielle doesn't wear "needy pink." She doesn't have to. She is needy pink personified. A conversation with her begins normally. That's her hook. Each time you see her you find yourself wondering *What was I thinking? She's not needy. She's an interesting individual.* However, depending on her self-esteem that day, in seconds to minutes, pernicious neediness starts to ooze.

Watch for a Needy Alert. A YELLOW ALERT is a compliment that turns into an obligation—maybe a small favor, an opinion, or an invitation to something you don't want to attend. *It was so nice of you to say those things about my art. Would you come to my opening on Friday? I must admit I'm a little nervous. It would mean so much to me if you came. You would add such an air of prestige to the showing.*

An ORANGE ALERT can come as a thank you or an unexpected gift with hidden strings attached. It most often is an expensive something that you didn't ask for, might not want, and possibly have no use for. Watch for the favor, opinion, or invitation to something you'd rather not attend that follows.

A RED ALERT is a more direct assault that casts you as her savior. It's phone calls about how no one wants to date her, though she makes no effort to meet anyone who might. This Needy Danielle behavior is called 'stalking' in street language.

I moved quickly. I found my way back to the protection of my childhood oak tree. But Needy Danielle had spotted and followed me. I'm a needy magnet.

At the tree, Danielle updated me on her life. She had a good job, but she needed a better one. She had a nice boyfriend, but she needed a nicer one. She had a cool apartment, but she needed a cooler one. She needed to see more of me. ALERT. She needed to know what I've been doing. ALERT.

I started to answer, but . . . She needed to tell me about how she needed to have surgery on her little finger to remove a hangnail.

She wanted to know how my work is going, but . . . she needed to tell me how her brother stuck her for the full bill at dinner last Friday night.

She needed to know what I think of her sweater, her pants, her shoes, her hat.

"Your hat?" I said. "It's . . . uh . . . most intriguing, but I'm wondering why a *feathered* hat in this humidity?" Darn, sucked in again. My mistake was to make a comment, which led to more needs. Did I think she needed to get rid of the hat? Did she need a hat at all? Did she need a new haircut instead? Maybe she needed a makeover. What did I think she needed?

Just as I was about to drown in that certain shade of pale pink, a familiar dog with caramel-colored eyes ran up to me. He jumped onto my lap, knocking me over on my imported riverbank. I collapsed laughing with relief and gratitude. This was no intrusion. This was rescue. The cavalry had come to save me.

"Sorry," said a baritone voice I now recognized without looking up. "He gets excited when he sees a beautiful woman."

"Shush," I said. "Where have you been?" Though we had no plan to meet, this was the best response for Needy Danielle to hear. I was fairly certain Larry would play along. "Larry, this is Danielle. Danielle, this is Larry. We were about to—"

"—walk the dog," Larry finished for me, perceiving my sense of urgency. He reached out to help me up and turned to Danielle to say. "Thanks for keeping Angela company."

"Angela?" Danielle said, stupefied. "Her name is . . . "

We smiled as we walked away, dog in tow.

As we walked, the dog made it clear that he was playing the role of a dog in tow solely for the benefit of our audience. It was also clear that he was thinking he deserved an Oscar for his performance. He did.

"How did you develop this uncanny habit of showing up at just the right time?" I asked as we walked into the Bean.

"You taught me years ago," he said.

"Did I also teach you to leave an envelope inside my first edition?" I asked, certain the drawing I found was his doing. "Where did you get it? I don't remember anything like it."

"I didn't get it. You drew it . . . the night you walked to the harvest moon with your dad. For safekeeping, you put it under your sweaters in the bottom drawer of your big chest," he reminded me. "I'm not sure when you found it. I guess you put it in the book so that it didn't get lost."

"How did you know I drew it? I didn't mention what was in the envelope," I stated, believing I had him cornered.

"How did I know you drew it? How do I know anything about you? You told me," he grinned. "The rest is on a need to know basis. And you don't *need* to know. Do you? You're not thinking you'd look good in needy pink?"

"Me? Needy pink? Never!" I asserted, feeling just a tiny bit needy, until his reflection in the Bean made me laugh.

Chapter Thirteen

Random Search Thinking

STANDING IN CLOUD GATE, Larry, the dog, and I quickly became like the other people—so many monkeys looking at the shiny weird surfaces trying to locate our shiny weird reflections so that we could make shiny weird faces at each other. As one might suspect, the dog was the most proficient at this little game. Our conversation, what little we had, centered on what we saw. The dog was uninterested in any conversation. Had I detected a hint of vanity in the dog?

At one point I stopped. I was stunned to realize that I was in my head. I was visiting the whole of Millennium Park in my head, with a thought of a person and a thought of a dog, standing inside a thought of the Bean to get away from a thought of Needy Danielle. We were surrounded by a crowd of other thought people who were doing the same thing—maybe not the part about avoiding Needy Danielle. That's a lot to have going on in my head.

I wondered where the rest of the information in my head had gone to make room for this much data. I confided in my reflection that I was curious how I could still be awake when my brain was producing a major motion picture in my head. Watching as my reflection became more disproportional, I figured that I must be awake, because I still heard the music on my playlist, even though I had left my headphones in the branches of my oak tree.

While I was doing these mental mathematics, Larry and the dog had tired of the Cloud Gate and its weird reflections. They had wandered off in the direction of the Crown Fountain.

The fountain was the other big draw of the park. Its two fifty-foot black, glass-block towers use LED technology to project video images of the faces of 1,000 Chicago citizens. The faces smile, twitch, smirk, and every fifteen minutes or so, spurt water from their mouths onto a concave surface to delight the awaiting crowd. Spanish artist Jaume Plensa had conceived the fountain in the tradition of water-spouting gargoyles.

I had never made friends with gargoyles in general, nor had I bonded with the Crown Fountain the way most people had.

I looked for man and dog near the fountain. Not seeing them, I headed back to my riverbank and white oak tree. I leaned against the tree and hugged my knees near my chest. In the comfort of that familiar space, I could observe people or I could think. I could think about anything or nothing— whatever I wanted.

Lately, thinking whatever I wanted was a luxury. At work, I spent my days solving other people's problems. At home, I spent my night solving my own problems—those that I hadn't begun to solve that day at work. When I was done solving my problems, I answered work email for an hour or so and attended to any project that needed special attention. Then I put together a list of 11 additional problems I needed to tackle the following day.

If I had brain power left, I answered email from friends. My replies were short. It takes energy to pass on details. At some point shortly thereafter my eyes glazed over, and all I was good for was mindless computer games that involved colors and shapes—no words.

This past Friday, however, I had been placed on direct orders from my boss, Benny Dietrich, to leave work at work. In another mandate, he had said I must use the weekend to find "balance." Using a suspiciously soft and caring voice, he said he thought I was working too hard and that he was worried I might fall apart from all that overachieving.

Why he thought *he* could decide what *I* would do on the weekend, I wasn't sure. But that was his way. When he wanted something, he spoke as if all was good and you were golden. When he didn't need you, you became part of the pavement.

Dressed in his khaki pants and fashion shirt, always monogrammed B.B.D. (a monogram I had translated to Barely Benevolent Dictator), Benny professed to have my best interests in mind when he told me to take the weekend off. He had professed this when he told me to uninvite Craig to the party.

I had noticed that the timing of Benny's professions of support had a certain predictability. Praise and support occurred when my unique skill set met his urgent needs for those selfsame skills.

I wondered what work would greet on Monday morning.

In his book, *Who Moved My Cheese?* Spencer Johnson had explained change in business and in life. In Benny's world, the cheese would be Swiss. His attitude would be "Throw out the cheese. I'm moving the holes."

Benny engineered situations guaranteed to make people fail. Factions disagreed on whether he did this to "thrive on chaos" or to keep everyone off balance. (There's that *balance* word again.) Most days I didn't care.

This day, the rebel in me—or was it the obedient worker?—had decided that whatever Benny's motives, I was going to have a weekend. He could call it balanced or unbalanced, but it would be without work.

I tried to think of the last time I had gone 24 hours without actually doing work. Slowly reality had become that I worked almost 24/7. The work was good, but I was so focused on a job well done that work was the only thing that I ever did well. I had edited out my life. Work was all I was.

The rest of my life wasn't good. In some ways, it wasn't there. Relationships were crumbling all around me. More than balance, I needed space. I needed that space to make room for a life. I was taking a weekend to not even think about work. Hopefully it was a step in the right direction.

There I was racing down the Sunday afternoon stretch and darn if I hadn't started to stumble. Thoughts of Benny had interrupted my weekend. I didn't need him to tell me to take the weekend off. I knew I worked too hard.

Technically, I might work for Benny, but I didn't *do my work* for Benny. I hadn't edited out my life for Benny. I did that for me. I got a charge out of a job done superlatively well.

Unfortunately, once again, the overachiever in me had started to think about work. I found myself on the horns of a dilemma. I had made a commitment to myself not to work this weekend. Yet, I knew if I thought about what was waiting for me on Monday I would be lost. The urge to get a jump on the week would be far too powerful to resist. Thinking about nothing wasn't an option now the attraction of work was in the air.

I needed something to think about, and I needed it now. I put my thinking on random search. I fixed my eyes on the first thing I saw. I literally let my eyes decide. Of course what I saw was Millennium Park. I thought about Millennium Park.

When I left Chicago it was the twentieth century. Millennium Park didn't exist. What did exist was a nondescript area of unused railway tracks, short city streets, and the underground Grant Park Parking Garage that served the loop at reasonable rates—though it was a little scary to use it at night. The area was unnamed, open, unremarkable, and leaning toward unsightly.

In honor of the new century, the city developed a plan to extend Grant Park north to include and dress up the proverbial step-child at the family reunion. With great fanfare, city philanthropists commissioned world-renowned architects, city planners, designers, and landscapers. They named their new baby Millennium Park and it was touted as the most significant millennium project in the world.

I tried for minutes to recall the pre-Millennium Park topography. But the old was so old, so inherently forgettable, and the new was so new, so visually engaging that the new had simply overwritten the old. Highlight, delete, cut, paste, done—a millennium miracle.

Gone were the unsightly railroad tracks and city blocks of nothing. Gone, too, was the history. Were they trying to erase what had happened here in 1968?

Like people, living spaces, even joyous living spaces such as Millennium Park, have a past. The history of this space was one of sadness, confusion, and unrest. That spring and early summer, Martin Luther King, and Bobby Kennedy had been assassinated. American boys were dying in Vietnam. Protesters gathered in Chicago to send a message to the Democratic Party during their national convention.

A jealous guardian of his city, Mayor Richard J. Daley had no sympathy for misbehavior. He arranged a show of force— 12,000 police on the street with the Illinois National Guard. Network television cameras recorded a bloody riot that injured more than 200 police and demonstrators. The country saw feelings out of control.

I looked at the beautiful park before me. Who'd imagine such an ugly event so near where I now sat? I guessed that most people visiting the park—real or imagined—weren't old enough or interested enough to know the history of where they stood. Heck, I was a clueless kid at the time.

I realized it wasn't the most uplifting think I'd ever had. It could have been worse. I could have found my way to nuclear holocaust.

That's what I get for putting the brain on random search thinking. Never know for sure what's going to bubble up. Still it *was* an emergency—a don't-think-about-work—situation.

Keep in mind: at the end of the day, you can walk away. I have to live in this head.

Meanwhile back at the oak tree, I sat thinking about what I had just been thinking. I suspected that my brain had gone far off track to avoid reviewing events of the past 24 hours. In the back of my mind, I again could hear my mother saying, "You don't even know this guy." In an itchy way, I was wondering whether I agreed with her, but wasn't sure I wanted to find out.

I had already decided that I liked Larry and his no name dog. Granted, they had appeared out of nowhere, but my hair follicles had gotten used to them. I didn't think about who I was when I was with them. I recognized that was a gift, rare and beautiful. Overall their presence in my life had been nonjudgmental, patient, generous, and kind.

Still, the relationship was not mutual. They knew things about me and I didn't know how they knew those things. Yet I knew next to nothing about them. Barring vague references that we had met before, and an eerie feeling of déjà vu, everything that I had picked up—all of it—I knew came from one day's experience. Larry wasn't exactly a free-flowing font of information. I had gotten more information from the dog.

They showed no signs of being stalkers, serial killers, or other such notorious villains. Larry was both generous and gentlemanly in every interaction. The dog had charisma in the way he brought clarity and wisdom.

But then there were Larry's fuzzy responses to my questions. He answered my questions as if I should know the answer.

Why does he always seem to be talking in code?

I needed to know what he was talking about. Asking him questions wasn't getting anywhere. I needed a new tack. I needed to coax him to change his behavior.

The best way to change someone's behavior is to change your own. Someone says something you don't like, something like "You're a pain." You don't like it, but you let it go. He moves on. It keeps happening the same way. Same action. Same response. He moves on.

Then one day he says "You're a pain," and you say "Thank you." Suddenly he has a new response to attend to. He is stopped, because you've changed your behavior. He has to change his. He doesn't move on. He offers a new response. What was a dance that occurred without thinking is now over. Variety sparks change.

Realizing that I still had my problem-solving skills on HIGH, I laid back. Reminding myself that it was still Sunday, I turned them OFF. I would not overthink answers about big 'L' Larry and his lowercase 'd' dog.

I chose the option that Larry had suggested in the concrete living room . . . *"Or you could accept a gift arranged with care in the spirit of generosity with which it was given."*

By accepting Larry and the dog without question, I could do both—change my behavior and stop overthinking.

If you want to stop limiting yourself, if you long to be someone else, change your mind.

It was a plan I could stay with at least through the weekend. I pulled my headphones out of the branches and listened to the playlist.

Larry and the dog wandered back. Larry was eating a corn dog. There was a substantial amount of French mustard dripping from the bottom of the corn dog onto his tan work boots. The dog was chewing what looked to be the T-bone from an expensive Chicago Porterhouse steak.

"It seems you two found yourselves a meal. Also looks like the dog got the better menu," I observed.

"Yeah, he blew all of our charisma at the back door of the Park Grill," smiled Larry. "So I was left begging at the kiosk. The mustard's superior though. Can I get you something?"

"No, thanks," I demurred. "I never eat on an empty head."

Dog and man sat down on the sloped grass of the riverbank next to me. Larry laid back to enjoy the same view of the passing clouds that I was seeing. In theater and in life, this is good blocking for serious conversation, side-by-side without looking at each other—close, but not confrontational. But we weren't talking. I was listening to music. He was petting the dog. We were both looking at the sky.

I was deep into Simon and Garfunkel's *Scarborough Fair/ Canticle,* watching clouds navigate the sky. I was rising and falling with the sounds as if cruising with the clouds. The voices were just so many more sound clouds going by.

Music is so many experiences at once—part reflective, part kinesthetic, part prayer, part nostalgic—always a totally new experience in each moment, every time.

I was surprised to find how nice it was to just be. I was having this thought when Larry next spoke.

"You look angelically peaceful. What are you thinking?"

I raised a hand to signal that I was far away and touched Larry's hand to let him know that I'd be back. I set his question on top of the peace I was feeling. I was thinking of nothing. I just was.

When the song was over, I collected my thoughts as I packed up my headphones and stuck them in the branches of the tree.

"Let's go for a walk," I said.

Chapter Fourteen

A Stand-Alone Verb

I LED LARRY AND THE DOG in the direction of my favorite part of the park—the Frank Gehry Pedestrian Bridge. From there you could see the city, the lake, the entire park, the gardens.

"I'd follow you anywhere," Larry said with a smile. The dog looked ready to go exploring.

"But you're not getting out of the question, just by taking me for a walk," Larry said, looking pleased with himself enough to be almost dancing. The dog hardly paid attention.

"I wasn't trying to avoid your question," I replied, turning my head to look him straight in the eye as we walked. "I just thought you might enjoy seeing more of the park while we talked. I know I would."

"Stalling for time, are you?" Larry said.

"No, replying to your last jibe. Interrupting again, are you?"

"No, just trying to knock you off your stride. Is it working?"

"Not really, but it was a valiant try." The dog appeared to be barely tolerating us, as if he were a bored babysitter.

"I didn't think so, but thanks for the support," Larry replied. "Where are we headed?"

"The bridge," I said mysteriously.

"Sounds musically symbolic," he played along.

"Oh it is." I played the moment to the hilt. "I never asked. Have you been to the park before? Have you seen the bridge?"

"That would be a no and a no," Larry answered.

"That would be a cool and a way cool," I laughed. Larry laughed too. The dog liked it when we laughed.

As we approached the bridge I was, as every time, taken by the flowing curves of stainless steel and hardwood. I couldn't help myself. My eyes ran over the length of it like a concert pianist practicing runs on the piano of my dreams.

"Ooo, look at those lines. Let your eyes follow the lines and you can't help but relax," I said. "Those are the lines of nature, of mathematics, of dance, of simplicity. But even better, this bridge is beauty with brains."

"Ladies and gentlemen," Larry began, "Step right up. For only a quarter see the mysterious flowing bridge with a brain. It walks. It talks. It crawls on its belly like a lizard."

Laughing at his carnival barker routine, it dawned on me that I couldn't remember when I played like this last. I knew it had been a long time. This was a feeling I had totally forgotten. Laughter and the freedom that comes with being silly. Our babysitter dog appeared to have gone from bored to disapproving. He moved to the other side of the bridge. To an unobservant passerby, it would appear that he was with some kids across the bridge.

Once we collected ourselves from our companionable giggle, we took a place along the inner side of the bridge overlooking the Pavilion. I continued where I'd left off.

"What I was trying to say was that I'm all for beauty, but I believe that form follows function. Most people don't realize that this gorgeous walkway also serves as an acoustical barrier. It's a castle wall protecting the enchanted Jay Pritzker Open Air Pavilion below from the noise of the dragons passing on Lake Shore Drive. Because of this bridge, the listening experience of the twenty-first century technological wonder is exquisite and magical."

"I never took you as someone who could sell a bridge, but if you ever need a second job . . . ," Larry started. "I'd buy it."

We both took a few minutes just leaning on the bridge and taking in the views in all directions. Apparently the dog had decided that we were no longer misbehaving, because he joined us again.

"So," Larry finally said. "Back to the question: what was making you look so peaceful?"

"I just was," I answered.

"That's not an answer."

"The thought I was having when you asked the question was how surprised I was at how nice it is just to be."

"What are you talking about?" Larry asked. "You know sometimes it's like everything you say has another meaning, and I don't know the code. The words make sense, except I don't know the secret. I'm missing something."

Did he really just say that? That was my thought. Those were my lines. Did he really feel that way? Or was he telling me that he knew I was feeling that way? STOP. No overthinking this afternoon.

"We've got the time, let's start from the beginning," I said. "In the 1950s and 60s Abraham Maslow introduced us to what he called the hierarchy of human needs. People move up Maslow's Hierarchy of needs; as they fulfill one set of needs, they work on the next. As a culture we've moved from *physiological needs*—things like food, clothing and shelter—to *safety needs* to *need for love and belonging*. We'll always be working on those for everyone, but we know what they're about. In the twentieth century, we did our holy best to make sure that everyone in the U.S. had a daily dose of self-esteem. We even made it part of our grade school curriculum."

"Yeah, that whole self-esteem thing has started to get on my nerves," Larry said. A big woof from the dog said he was right with us on that one. I guess we all had spent too much time in the company of kids who had too much self-esteem and not enough respect for others.

"I'm thinking that this century is destined to be the century of self-actualization. Or, as I've been thinking of it, the century of *becoming obsessed with becoming.* Self-actualization is about becoming being the best you can be, but it is not actually getting there. The minute you get there, you are no longer self-actualizing. You are there—you ARE the best you can be."

"It certainly seems like we don't need anything more for people to obsess about," Larry commented. He was leaning on his arms over the rail looking back at me. The dog had decided to sit for a while since we didn't seem to be going anywhere in the near future.

"Well, that's kind of my point and gets us one step closer to answering your question. I'm about as self-actualizing as they come. Curious people are—that's what makes them curious. But you know, sometimes, I don't want to be becoming better. Sometimes I just want to be me. Maslow left that out of his hierarchy. Sometimes we just need to be."

I turned my back to the rail of the bridge to take in the city skyline. The view of the city was refreshing and invigorating. The dog turned with me. Apparently he thought so too.

"So that's what you were trying to tell me? That you were just being? That's what gave you that look of peace?" Larry asked skeptically, still not convinced that the thin slice of difference in how I was using the language really existed. The dog, however, definitely a master at knowing how to be and knowing how just to be, was right with me.

"Larry, I've studied linguistics and grammar, and I'm fascinated by people and behavior. The English language falls short in describing the act of just be-ing—just allowing one's self to exist. There should be a lesson in grammar books about the value of the verb be as a stand-alone verb, as opposed to its role as a linking or copulative verb, like this:

I am.	*You are.*	*He is.*
	We are.	*She is.*
		It is.
		They are.

I was.	*You were.*	*He was.*
	We were.	*She was.*
		It was.
		They were.

"As I recall, there already is such a lesson," he said.

"It looks like there's one, but there isn't. Unfortunately, in the English language, if you say 'I am. You are', you get the question, 'You are what?' and that's the problem.

"In a world of stress and overachievers looking for balance, it seems a stand-alone verb, *be*—a word that underscored the ability just to be—is desperately needed. So that if you say, 'I am', you get the answer, 'Wow, that's great!'

"I can see the sample lesson now." I turned around to use the air in front of us as an invisible whiteboard. I wrote and said:

> *I was. I am. I still am.*
> *Hopefully I am getting better.*

"That one would be crossed out. Instead it would say something like this:"

> *Hopefully I find more time to just be.*

I wrote in the invisible white board and said it aloud.

I continued. "We used to have that meaning of the word *be*. When did we give it up?" I turned to Larry, appealing in earnest. "Our immigrant grandparents used it all of the time when they said, 'Oh, just let me be.'"

Unconsciously, I just started walking. It wasn't very polite of me. When I realized it, I stopped and turned back, but I didn't have to. Larry and the dog were right beside me.

"What do you say we head back to the tree and just see what we want to be?" Larry said with a smile. "Unless you'd like me to make a spectacle of myself on the bridge again."

"Nah, you did that already."

"Yeah, but it made you laugh," he said. The dog recognized the banter and slowly started putting some distance between himself and us.

"Yeah, it sure did," I smiled. "I sure did."

We took a different way back, cutting through the Pavilion so that we could peek at the gardens.

"You said the sky gives you a sense of space, of having a place in the universe without anyone judging you. Is that how you feel now?" Larry asked me.

I looked up from a flower to answer Larry's question. "Yes, gardens, trees, anything in nature. Music does it too. They all give me a sense of space. They tell my place and part in the universe. Buildings and people contain me in ways that this flower, the lake, and the sky do not."

"Spoken like a true angel," was all he said, and the three of us headed back to the tree, each of us thinking our own thoughts in the kind of silence easily shared with friends.

Maybe it was time to expand the balance rule again.

> *Be curious about everything. Don't overthink anything. Take an equal dose of color for every word you see, hear, or say. Find space and perspective through music and in nature. Try to think more about less.*

When we settled ourselves on the riverbank once again, it was Larry with his back against the tree, looking out at the people, the dog beside him, and me on my back looking up through the leaves.

"Do all buildings and all people contain you or just some buildings and some people?" Larry asked, picking up the conversational thread that we had left at the garden.

Had to give him that one. It would have been my next question. I thought before I answered. I knew my answer would be no—not all. I wanted to decide whether it would be a big no or a little no.

The dog came over beside me. I tousled the fur on his head, what there was of it, a thank you for his moral support.

My answer was a memory. "I remember when I went to college, I went to the bank to open a checking account. The bank was in a landmark building. While I was standing behind the velvet rope waiting my turn, I saw a little girl sitting on the marble floor near her mother playing quietly with her dolls. I identify with that little girl."

"Buildings can be a fabulous place to find a sense of space.
That little girl had made that space her own. That bank lobby
was high ceilings and tall pillars, replete with surfaces that
offered plenty of tactile feedback. No one had asked the little
girl to get up. So the space was friendly—nonjudgmental. I
could lose myself in a place like that. People can build elegant,
safe places that remind us that God is in His heaven, and
angels are everywhere."

"It would seem then that churches would be such a place," he
offered. "Old elegant churches anyway."

"I can lose myself in an old church—not every old church,"
I said. "Some are cold, damp relics. Sometimes I find heaven
in a new one—one where I feel free to touch the furniture and
to breathe in the life of the space. I had that experience in
the cathedral in Pasadena. Though I didn't find it physically
beautiful, I felt a sense of closeness to God, a freedom from
judgment. A guy visiting the church asked my friend if I had a
furniture fetish, because I was touching everything. I've felt the
same thing in buildings of beauty and form of many kinds."

"Beautiful buildings bring out our humanity," Larry added.
"Good architects seem to know that. You can feel it when you
walk into their buildings, I think." The dog lifted his head in
agreement. It was ironic to be having this conversation under
a tree on a riverbank with a backdrop of Chicago's skyline of
towering buildings and the foreground of the park, the water
and the sky.

"Still, it's hard to be a grown-up version of that little girl
without suffering repercussions," I said. "I know I've learned
to edit my responses defensively. The sky, any part of nature,
these are okay for grown-ups to explore. Buildings require
reconnaissance before you get too involved in experiencing

them. Feng Shui is not an American idea. Nor is sitting on marble floors past the age of reason. Choose incorrectly and you'll quickly be reminded that you are acting in a way that is inappropriate for a grown person to behave. Being different is a greater sin than theft in some circles. Certainly it can be a greater threat to an ordered world."

"How does your sense of space work with people?" Larry asked.

"Are you writing a book?" I asked.

"You have an interesting way of interacting with the world," Larry coaxed. The dog gave that get-on-with-it look, and I did.

"My friends offer me space," I said. "I can be who I am without judgment. I like who they see when they look at me. I feel like I'm in a no-edit zone. I just am.

"But most people are especially tricky. Like wildebeests in the Serengeti, they must be approached with care or the result is a VERY judgmental response. Some want to share who they are; others find any observation an intrusion. Telling which is which is complicated."

"People are funny that way," Larry said. "They all walk around wanting to be loved, but they wait for the other guy to do it."

"I'm beginning to think that many people—maybe me too— unconsciously use subterfuge to confuse anyone who might try from figuring out whether we want to share who we are. What if we share too much of who we are and then get judged unfit or unworthy, because we chose to share with the wrong guy? What if we don't share enough and get judged as cold and unfeeling? Being a person is hard enough. Sharing is scary stuff. Getting to know some of us can be close to impossible."

"Why do people learn to be so scared and so scary?" Larry wondered. The dog just looked bewildered and forlorn.

"Who knows? We're a weird species." I stopped to think. "I'm sure that little girl hadn't figured it out yet. Bet she had no opinion whatsoever about what the grown-ups were doing in that lobby. She probably just figured they were grown-ups, that's what they do. That's sort of how I look at people. Each of them does what they do, however they do it. Who am I to judge? I'm weird enough in my own way—after all, I'm sitting on the marble floor too, whenever I can. But somewhere in that group of grown-ups is someone who doesn't approve of that little girl."

Suddenly, I didn't feel so good about what I had been saying. I heard my mother saying I'm too open with people. That it's wrong to wear my feelings on my sleeve. I started to feel anxious as if I had hurt someone's feelings or made someone angry. It's what happens when I talk about my feelings to someone who hasn't said enough about his own.

At times like this it was hard not to think my mother was right—feelings are weakness. Everything I'd said was true, but I felt like I'd done something horribly wrong. Larry might be the one who disapproves of little girls who sit on the floor.

I was a giant stand-alone verb—was.

What the situation called for was an action verb.

"You know, Larry," I said. "I've probably said enough. I'm going to head back. I need to do things before work tomorrow." This time I knew that tomorrow was Monday.

"Sure," Larry said, helping me gather my oak tree and the riverbank on which it stood. "Thanks for sharing your feelings.

Don't worry, they're safe with me. When you start to overthink this conversation, remember I'm the guy who brought a dog into the International Flagship Club at the airport."

How did he know about that?

"Yeah, but that was a dream," I said.

"Hey," Larry said, looking me right in the eye. "I've sat on a few marble floors myself."

The dog, however, just gave me a pensive look.

Did that look mean they were part of the dream? Did that mean that he didn't approve? Was I getting paranoid over a canine's opinion of human behavior?

As I ran home, I left out everything between the park and the driveway to my building. I stayed in my head through a half-hearted walk up the driveway to ease the transition before I opened my eyes. Then with eyes open, I sat at my desk staring at the stuffed penguin on my bookcase.

I wasn't really thinking. I was just staring, trying to repack my feelings back inside myself. But they weren't folding up the way they should. A new sense of déjà vu was creeping over me.

I barely recognized that my phone was ringing, a mere two inches from my right hand. It was Isaac at the front desk. He was calling to say I had a delivery—a package.

I rode the elevator down, too aware of who might have sent me a package. I picked up the package. For a moment, I froze as Isaac handed it over to me. It was a small box, addressed by computer but, like the envelope, there was no stamp.

Isaac said, "Hope you don't mind that I called you again about it. I thought you might need it. I didn't want you to forget it was here."

Of course not! This box was various items I had ordered from the pharmacy on Broadway. They deliver. I *had* forgotten this package, which had arrived on Friday. Larry's comment about bringing a dog to the airport—straight out of my movie-plot dream—had triggered a returning sense of déjà vu whispering in my ear. I had worked myself up to believing this package would reveal another something I couldn't explain.

Heading back up, Mini-Cooper girl got on the elevator with me, but I hardly noticed her. I simply stared at the package all the way up to my floor. I walked to the apartment. I opened the door, and went straight to my letter opener with the star at the top. I used it to open the package. Everything was exactly what I'd ordered—nothing less and more importantly, nothing more.

I thought maybe that poem about being bothered might help me bring myself back to the ground. I pulled out my poetry folder. Once again, I read the poem *Bother* aloud, but I was still bothered by that creeping sense of déjà vu. Mindlessly, I started to page through that poetry folder. Then, in the back, I saw it—something that didn't belong. An unlined page stuck out a little wider than the others. It sat behind the composition book of "Mostly Poor Poetry from My Youth."

Using two fingers I pulled out another child's drawing. This showed one of my favorite places—the Chicago Cultural Center. I'd been to the Cultural Center many times since I was a child. I'd been there before it was the Cultural Center, when it was still the Chicago Public Library. I'd been there many times with family, with friends in high school, college, and beyond.

This drawing was titled "Me, Larry, and the dog." We were sitting on the marble floor in the Cultural Center. But I'd never been there with Larry and the dog. How did I draw this. Did I make it up? Did I dream this too?

The drawing had something else—a PAW PRINT. It looked as if a dog had stepped on it. You could almost imagine that a dog had signed it.

I could take it to mean that the dog approved after all.

Chapter Fifteen

Splinters

I DIDN'T NEED ANOTHER SHOWER, but I took one anyway. I wanted to wash away my confusion and anxiety. I had done too much talking to Larry about things that make me uncomfortable. Every conversation I had about feelings found its way back to me—my feelings twisted, torn, and totally unrecognizable. I didn't need a memory of my mother to tell me that I was vulnerable for having shared my feelings again.

Added to that was the drawing of the Cultural Center. Though possibly a vote of support or simply a forgotten memory, it held its own mystery. I'd just gotten used to a guy who knew my past and could predict my future, but now his dog was getting into the act? I knew that even this exceptional dog couldn't hold crayons. My brain needed a restart, but a shower was all that I had.

Once again, I let the water drench me, expand me, and release me. Stress washed away, leaving a sense of wellbeing. When I finally finished the shower, I was again, for a split second, the cleanest person in the universe.

My body felt refreshed. My mind felt hungover with anxiety, as if I had had too much alcohol and done something terribly embarrassing in public. I stayed in my huge terrycloth bathrobe and pulled the hood over my head for protection. I sought out another mindless task to feel like I'd accomplished something.

Though it was early Sunday afternoon, and I hadn't yet decided what to wear today, I went straight to my closet to choose what to wear to work on Monday. I stood staring blankly waiting for my clothes to talk to me. I stared blankly like this every time I faced this painful ritual.

Which do I pick first—pants or top? What if I picked one and couldn't decide on the other? What if I pick a perfect outfit and then decide that it's a better choice for Tuesday? Has it been too soon? Will anyone remember this outfit from the last time I wore it?

I picked up a pad and pencil. I listed and surveyed what every-one had worn to work for the past three weeks. I knew I was endowing the world with a great deal more interest in my fash-ions than they actually had. But I figured the point at which I couldn't remember what *they* wore was the only safe guess.

It's not that I have no taste. Nor do I lack imagination, elegant apparel, or the ability to put the pieces together without little coded animal tags. I was damaged by childhood fashion deprivation.

Events beyond my control had squelched my natural talent.
The tragedy—school uniforms—had occurred when I was
in third grade. At the time, I, like so many other poor waifs,
had gone along with the idea, as if we were lining up for
candy. Young as we were, we naively had envisioned our
entire school wearing elaborate costumes not unlike those
of the Swiss Guard. We were far enough from big city schools
with uniforms to have no idea of what this uniform thing
was about. Instead of Swiss Guard fancy, we got plain white
shirts, navy blue pants and skirts, and navy blue cardigan
sweaters. Boring.

Parents were thrilled. Wardrobe costs dropped significantly.
Competition over cool clothes was squashed before it
started—another huge savings. Bonus prize: kids didn't waste
time in the morning deciding what to wear. Of course, once
this kid grew up and did have to decide what to wear each day,
she didn't know how. Little did parents realize the life skills
their children were losing.

So, that Sunday like so many Sundays before, I stood staring
at my closets wishing I had already made a decision. I yearned
for a sweatshirt I once saw that read *Give me ambiguity or give
me something else*. The fear stood with me. If I didn't make my
apparel choice in advance, one morning I would freeze and die
of indecision.

> **HEADLINE NEWS:** *Modern-Day Woman Found
> Turned to Stone at Closet Door While Trying to
> Decide What to Wear. Tune in Tonight at 11.*

In the end, I chose a walnut green, long flowing dress
that buttoned down the front with a tan silk jacket and a

cream-colored, woven t-shirt bought with birthday money Grandma sent. I hadn't worn that since last year—safe on that count. I have two more jacket dresses and two similar long dresses, so the rest of the week is covered. It was a load lifted to know that at least this wouldn't be nagging at my brain the rest of the day.

They say that Albert Einstein had numerous shirts that were exactly the same. Steve Jobs had his piles of black turtlenecks. I thought about that, but I knew I was no Einstein or Jobs. The only viable solution seemed to be that when I hired a person to sort my photos, I might extend the contract to include laying out my clothes for the next day. That could work.

The distraction of choosing what to wear had helped for the while I was making that decision. But the anxiety about my conversation with Larry had returned. Now again, I was replaying what I'd told him about my feelings. I busied myself with getting my apartment in order, even organizing my closet. Getting things in order wasn't working. I was still in my bathrobe. I wandered around my apartment. Wandering wasn't working either.

I knew I could take over-analyzing to an art form. I wondered why that was so. About then I realized that I was feeling vulnerable over a conversation that had taken place *in my head.*

I decided that maybe I was spending too much time in my head. People were going to think I was crazy. I needed airing out. I needed to walk. No question about that. The question was where to go.

I'd think about where while I got ready to go. I threw off the terrycloth bathrobe and got ready to face the real world head on. I put on my jeans, a beefy white t-shirt, a favorite washed-out denim shirt over it, no socks, and plain old ordinary sneakers. I laced up the sneakers.

Then in a moment's perfect synchronicity my eyes fell on the keys that Richard had given me. . . . My mind pulled the moment back so clearly.

⊰⊱   ⊰⊱   ⊰⊱

He placed the keys in my hand. "Here you go, evil twin-girl, party or hide, as you will. I suspect you'll do more of one than the other." He winked.

I looked at the keys in my hand in bewilderment and surprise. I loved Richard that much. I would miss him dearly. I was already looking forward for the day when he would be back. His brain, his humor, his generosity, all of whom he has made the world a better place. It never crossed my mind he might feel the same about me.

⊰⊱   ⊰⊱   ⊰⊱

This was one time I didn't need an operations manager. I knew exactly what to do. I went to the kitchen, made two peanut butter sandwiches with raspberry preserves, poured some cold milk in an extra water bottle, and grabbed some paper napkins. I wrapped the sandwiches and carefully added my lunch to the usual contents of my writer's backpack. Then I picked up my backpack, grabbed my phone and keys, and made sure I had my glasses and my wallet.

I was out the door and down the elevator in about five minutes. The biggest decision was whether to walk or take a taxi. I decided to walk.

Before I set off I put on my headphones and launched a new playlist. With a smile I set off. I couldn't help but think that the world was wondering what I was smiling about.

I walked to the beat of the music. I danced to the beat of the music (when no one was looking and sometimes when they were). I felt the real breeze off the lake on my very real face as I heard the real music in my real ears, smiling at the real people I passed on the street.

As I walked down the street, I imagined that I was the heir to a fabulous fortune and that everyone I saw was someone I knew—old friends from the past who didn't recognize me. It made the walk a joyful experience. I smiled at everyone. I received a wealth of returned smiles and positive feedback from the people I passed on the street. It was almost as if the whole world was in on the game I was playing. People said hello and made room for me on the sidewalk. I felt like a celebrity. I half expected someone to ask for my autograph and started thinking about whose name I might scribble.

I got to Richard's restaurant about fifteen minutes later. I didn't feel bothered any more. I felt like I was on vacation—a vacation with a purpose.

First I had a little "prep work" to do.

I walked past the restaurant and went into Gunnar's flower shop. Gunnar wasn't there. He never was on Sundays. But Sherry was and she still recognized me.

"Hey, there!" she said. "On reconnaissance again, right?"

"Always," I said. Barely able to take my eyes away from the flowers, I looked up long enough to give her a big grin that let her know I saw her and that she was a person I liked a lot. "Testing, constantly testing," I said as I always did when I started to wander around the store. I was always overwhelmed by the choices.

Sherry knew the routine. I would take at least four tours before I picked up a flower. Then, like a banshee I'd pull them together into a colorful bunch. She was free to wait on as many customers as came in during the time I was there, because I was never in a hurry in a flower shop.

I went out to the flowers displayed on the sidewalk and into the cooler and out to the sidewalk and into the store and into the cooler and out to the sidewalk and around the store and into the cooler. I thought I had an idea by then, so I went back out to the sidewalk.

Out on the sidewalk, I pulled five gerbera daisies—three bright white, two bright yellow—and three deep blue delphiniums. In the cooler, I selected three flaming red lilies, three burning orange lilies, one white starburst lily, and three giant white peonies. This meant, of course, that I had to go back outside for at least three more deep blue flowers the name of which I never found out, and three bright red-orange gerbera daisies.

"So I see you're still a sucker for color," Sherry said, smiling. "You want me to trim these and add greens, I assume?" She had already started making them ready for water.

"You betcha," I said, looking around for an appropriate inexpensive container to suit my purposes.

"Looking for a vase, are you?" Sherry finished trimming them. She then added greens to suit her taste and mine.

"You know all of my secrets, don't you?" I said with a grin.

"Here. This is one we don't really need," Sherry said giving the grin right back.

"You're the best! How much do I owe you?"

"Well, let's see, with Gunnar's discount . . . " She figured and calculated a little bit and then passed a piece of paper my way. It was a deal.

"Worth it at twice the price," I said. "I'm coming back here more often."

"Wish you would," she said. "We miss you."

"You know, I miss you too," I said, and I hadn't really realized it until I'd said it. I felt a tinge of loss as I walked out the door.

Still I was on a mission. I walked two doors back the way I had come and turned left into the hotel hallway. Then with a sincere thank you sent across the airwaves to Richard and a solemn mental ceremony, I set down the vase, pulled out the keys, and unlocked the door to the restaurant.

It was about then that I realized I didn't know how to turn on the lights.

As luck would have it, the switch was right where anyone would expect it to be. I picked up the vase, closed the door, and locked it behind me. Then I carried the vase over to the copper bar, unloaded the lunch part of my backpack, and got ready to spend the next 45 minutes arranging flowers while I listened to music.

When the recording industry realized there was money to be made in re-releasing old vinyl LPs, I took on the quest of rebuilding my music collection. My most favorite LPs had been ruined years ago by a foundation leak in an apartment I once rented, but despite their moldy and unusable condition, I had been unable to part with them. It took a while, but I finally converted them all to digital, taking care that the most important songs would be available on all of my devices.

At times of trouble I'd scroll through the soundtrack of my life: top 40s that played while my brother and I did dishes; songs on the radio when my dad taught me to drive; songs that marked high school and college. It took me a long time to realize as I found tune after tune that I hadn't been rebuilding a music collection: I was constructing a time machine.

I put my entire music library on shuffle and mindlessly started arranging flowers. I needed to look in on myself. I needed to get perspective about then, now, life, and me to rediscover bits of me—things I had forgotten in the rush to grow up, in the rush to succeed, little bits of who I am that are worth keeping.

Once the flowers were arranged, I sat down at the copper bar, pulled out my sandwiches and milk, and ate lunch.

Life is always better after peanut butter.

I cleaned up after lunch and thought this was not where I wanted to be.

"Close, but no cigar," I heard myself say aloud.

I gathered and repacked my belongings and made straight for the back door. I tested the key, checking twice to make certain that I could get back through the same door if needed. Then I held my breath and approached the ever-looming fire escape.

Maybe it was the daylight or that I had passed this way just last night, but I made it up the fire escape with only slight palpitations, despite the vase of flowers and the backpack. Again I was There. There I was.

This time I could enjoy being here and There. Last time I'd been frustrated, confused, and somewhat furious with Craig. I told Larry I was not so happy with the way he and his dog disrupted me, and their response was snores. This time, I had flowers and music, a full stomach, and my journal.

I sat on the long couch under the sky and I pulled out my phone. I added seven hours to the time on my phone and figured that Richard was probably still up but definitely not home that early. I dialed his number anyway. I got his voicemail.

"Richard darling, it's your evil twin. Just calling to say that I used your keys as you suggested and the flowers I bought looked beautiful on the copper bar. Oh yes, and I love you, darling."

I ended the call and made myself comfortable. I relished the thought that I would write under the cloudless blue of the afternoon sky. I hit play on Dan Fogelberg's Wild Places album. I thought he might have something to say to me, because we both grew up in Illinois. I let myself lay back on the couch, listening to him sing about heaven on earth and feeling like I owned every bit of the sky.

I decided to run home to see the oak tree on the riverbank in my backyard instead of bringing it to me.

Another advantage of running my way, I did the 90-mile trip in about 90 seconds, skipping the traffic on the expressways.

I started in the green grass about 30 yards away from the tree. I let the giant oak grow in my vision as I walked up to it, pretending I was a movie camera as I had done when I was a child. Then I hugged the old tree before I took my place next to it overlooking the river.

This was a great thinking, dreaming, learning tree. This was a place where I had always been able to be me. I leaned back until I was flat, looking at the sky through the leaves of the tree. Under this tree, the sky always looked friendlier to me.

I had only meant to stay long enough to breathe in the essence of that childhood place. I hadn't really posed a question, but I began to realize that I had been carrying an answer. I had been going at this quest for balance all wrong. I returned to the rooftop.

It was perfect that I was back in the concrete living room. I needed to be somewhere solid while I sorted out some sort of breakthrough. I needed to know I was in the real world with my eyes wide open.

Done with my run home, I opened my eyes. I stared at the blue canvas of the sky to sort out what I was thinking.

I had decided to make room for new thinking—that's not a small thing. It had taken a long time to get through all of the old think and past tape recordings that had kept me going. I was opening the windows of my brain.

Most people think establishing balance in life works like a balanced diet—you need so many of these, of that, and of those. Apply the same kind of rules and similar rigor to your lifestyle and you'll get a balanced life. My mind argued that doing that would only result in more prearranged activities and possibly more stress trying to fit them all in.

I'd been looking at balance all wrong. Balance speaks of nuance and blending, not organization and structure. When you put weights on a scale, it's how many, not how you organize them, that counts.

I found myself looking at my life as a birth-to-death whole. The things that filled me up—like the peace of sitting under the oak tree, the music I was listening to—were part of who I am. The things that took my energy—being anxious for talking about my feelings, following my boss's ludicrous requests—were tied to trying to be someone I was not.

Balance must be in comparing the people I used to be with the person I wanted to become. Balance is found in recognizing the parts worth keeping together.

Now that was a point of view worth making a friend. Had I always, in some way, known that? Is that why I brought the tree with me everywhere I ran?

I stopped the music. I set my headphones aside.

I took out my journal and my favorite pen, I began to write.

I'm not sure where the words came from, or how long I wrote. I know it wasn't long. Sometimes writing works like that.

When I was done, I had written a poem about my quest for balance. I gave this entry a title, "Splinters of My Self."

Splinters of My Self
Splinters of introspection
tiny ideas and mirrors of me
sparkle so sprightly
in the eyes of my mind
pointing the way to my calling
yet giving it no direction.

Splinters from searching a soul
so many slivers of silver and light
fit not so tightly
in the work of my life
sorting through splinters and falling
making it less than complete.

Wishing me forward on one pilgrim's journey
finding the way to my home
putting the pieces back in their places
reclaiming the self that is whole.

I read the poem over several times. I kept reading to figure out what I was trying to tell myself. Then, when I felt I knew, I wrote other entries in my journal. Then I closed my eyes simply to think.

The dog showed up about then. How he knew to come or that his company would be welcome was his magic. I read what I had written.

The ways that I have edited out my life are becoming apparent to me. I haven't been purposeful or dramatic, but in subtle ways I have distanced myself from my "self." I was too busy for email from friends. I couldn't make Jessie's wedding, Natalie's trip. I set this package here. I put that envelope there. I left my feelings with them. It was safer to have too much work than to have too many feelings.

Unconsciously I had broken off bits of my self, leaving them, losing them, or letting people borrow them, and I moved on. Some broke off by accident. Some were left in the care of others. Some were thrown away as no longer needed. Some were in storage, waiting for visits from me that I had never planned to make.

Once Katie had asked, "You've never pressed a flower, have you?"

"No," I had answered. "Then I'd have to keep it." That wasn't why. The reason was that pressed flowers bothered me. The real reason was the violets.

As I thought about it, I reached down to pet the dog. He rubbed his head against my hand. This was not a happy revelation. I think he knew.

I had set the pen down after I wrote that entry. I clearly remembered why pressed flowers bothered me.

⚹ ⚹ ⚹

I was on a hillside by my house picking rich, dark violets to give to my mother. I probably called her mommy then. The flowers were small, tiny really, smaller than me. It made me feel so big to hold them gently in my hand. I looked down on them for hours. I was lost in the velvety soft that was their petals and so surprised by the frail lightness that was their stems.

How did these delicate tiny friends survive the winters of the big kids tearing down the hill on old wooden, creaky sleds, leaving trails of wax and rust in their wake? "My goodness," is what I always imagined the woman in the white house across the street must have said when she saw that beautiful purple hillside.

I carried those flowers into the kitchen carefully and gave them proudly to my mother. She quickly put them in water in a paper cup on the counter. She said, "Thank you, honey. But don't bother to pick the violets. They don't last. I'll put them in water. When they die, we'll press them."

Then she walked into the living room. The beautiful flowers were drooping already, and so was I.

❧ ❧ ❧

Wild violets are still my favorite flower. But I never picked them again. I pulled the dog closer as I thought about it. He didn't seem to mind.

I kept my journal and my pen. I returned to the music, this time as I listened, I would listen until the words talked to me. Some people opened their Bible to find a message. I opened my music.

I leaned back and turned the volume up. As I did, I felt the lowercase 'd' dog lie down on the concrete beside me. I guessed he wanted to be my totem on this vision quest. I was glad for the company and ready to go where the experience took me.

I didn't close my eyes, but I focused inside—to my heart and my childhood. The music in my headphones seemed to move to my own drummer me as I wrote a path through my mind:

The drum of my heartbeat underscores the life that is meant to be mine.

The music over, the dog jumped up, two paws on the couch to see what I wrote. Like a small child who has completely accepted the illusion, I knew the dog read the page. The dog approved. In fact, if he could hold a pen, he would have underlined the last line.

Then I had to add one of my own.
It's time to see who you are.

I stayed with the dog under the sky. We shared that silence that two friends share with ease and comfort, free from worry over the other's thoughts.

The sentence
It's time to see who you are.

remained in front of me.

All photos of my childhood were carefully stored in three hard-to-access places—six actually—three places in my home and three more in the care of three friends. Now a seventh was the box next to my desk. My brother had recently sent me the box filled with photos he found when selling our father's business. That box was sitting on my mother's cedar chest, less than an arm's reach away from my desk.

It was time to go home and at least think about looking at those photos. I started to pack my stuff. The dog waited patiently. At that moment, he was the perfect date.

"Hello, Ma'am," a voice said, "Are you staying at the hotel again?"

I looked up. It was Armando. He was the young man who wanted to be a graphic designer. When I stayed in the hotel, I'd helped him with his Algebra.

"Hey, Armando! Ah, no, I'm not at the hotel. Just visiting. How are you?" I said, delighted to see him. "How are classes? What are you taking now?"

"Well, I made it through Algebra after you left. Thank you for your trick for remembering how to figure ratio, distance, and time," he grinned. "Now I'm trying to get through Algebra 2. I come here to study on my break."

"Let's take a look," I said. We worked together on the first few problems. Then I said, "Remember, if you're not getting it, it's because they haven't found the right way to explain it to you."

"Yeah, I remember," he said, "but I'm still confused."

"Hey," I said, right before Armando went in from his break. "Remember, Algebra is a lot less confusing than people. In Algebra, at least you stand a chance of finding a right answer." Armando laughed and said his good-bye.

When the sun got below the hotel's roof, I repacked my backpack, put it on, and picked up the flowers. Moving carefully, I went in through the window. The dog followed. When I got to the street, I let the dog walk me home. We didn't talk. He knew I had things on my mind. He was one of the things. Gentle-dog that he was, when we arrived at my building, he left me politely at the door and dissolved into the night.

When I walked in, I saw something in my mailbox. I carefully held the vase as I maneuvered the key and pulled it out. I ignored my surprise that anything was near my mailbox on a Sunday. Too spent to be curious, I slid it between my fingers and the vase without looking. Up the elevator and into the apartment. I set it aside while I went about arranging the flowers for their new home on the cabinet in the living room.

It was quite a while before I picked it up to see what had been hand delivered on a Sunday afternoon.

It was an ordinary business-size, bulk-mail envelope, addressed to me, apparently hand delivered. Inside was a beautiful, tri-fold brochure advertising events in Millennium Park.

The cover of the brochure was a shot of the Chicago skyline as reflected in the Bean. No people were in the photo. The photo had been taken in such a way as to show the reflections of many people, but not the people themselves. It was very cool.

Across the inside, the fully opened 11.5 inches showed a panoramic view including Pritzker Pavilion and the Geary Bridge. You could see a little boy and his mom looking up at the stage of the Pavilion. People on the bridge included a group of teenagers walking side-by-side, and a couple standing by the rail, talking. I also saw a dog standing near the opposite rail.

What I saw in the bridge photo made me pick up my magnifying glass to look at the reflections in the Bean photo more closely. Then I saw it, the reflection of a man, a woman, and a dog among the crowd of people. In the bridge photo, in the Bean photo, those people looked like Larry, the dog, and me. But we'd only been there in my head, and that was only this morning. Even Quickie Print couldn't print and deliver a brochure like that in so little time.

Surely this must be that sensitivity thing, where you start to see what you've been thinking about everywhere you look. What else could it be?

Chapter Sixteen

Smiles that Reached Out

IT WAS SUNDAY EVENING. I looked at my mother's cedar chest. A mysterious piece of furniture from my childhood, it had always been off limits. I never did know whether my mother had it before she married or my father had bought it for her. Either way, it had lost the luster of newlyweds.

It no longer held a wedding dress, linens for a new home, or the baby clothes from three children. Once it had held letters a soldier had written to her sister during the war. My mother had secreted the letters for mysterious reasons. I discovered the letters the year my mom died and gave them to my aunt on her birthday.

I considered how this chest, possibly the first piece of furniture my mother owned, had become one more in my collection of fine furniture. It was well-worn by the time it became mine. I used it for a printer stand, work surface, and storage. I checked the contents every five or six years when I moved from one city to another. Though the classic piece of furniture had been part of my family longer than I had, I showed it little respect and gave it no station.

People kept telling me to get rid of it. That was not an option. I had thoughts of refinishing it with black lacquer to give it a deco look. I once thought that might give it back some of the respect it demanded. Just when I'd gotten close to doing so, I'd decided that would ruin it. I'd come to view the marks it wore as deeply authentic.

I was painfully aware that I couldn't list the contents of the chest, even if it meant winning a game show. Larry had told me that the chest held my childhood drawings. Despite my great memory, I couldn't guess whether that was so. The chest had become the place where I put things that I wanted to keep, but forget about. Curious as I might be, I wasn't ready to open Pandora's box.

It was the box on the cedar chest that needed my attention.

Now was the time to open that box to go through the photos my brother had sent me. How many photos could there be? The box had been here for over a week. If I didn't open it soon it would become part of the furniture.

I picked up the box. The hard-cardboard box once held an expensive serving bowl for an elegant family dinner. I had a good idea what was inside now. The box held photos and souvenirs from my life. My brother had recently sorted through the boxes of photos and memorabilia he'd found when selling our father's business. He had sent me those he thought I'd want to keep.

I decided before taking out those photos that I needed something to eat. I opened the refrigerator to see what was there.

My refrigerator is famous among my friends who have seen inside it. After a moment of initial amazement, they can't quite understand how a full-grown human being could own a full-size refrigerator housing such a fully weird conglomeration of contents. It had become sport and tradition that the first event after hanging of coats and setting down of suitcases was that visitors opened the refrigerator to see what they might find this time.

I looked over the contents like a visitor. I saw scores of nutritional drinks in chocolate and butter pecan. Plenty of cheeses, grapes, bacon, cottage cheese, some peaches, hot fudge, chocolate sauce, cupcakes shared space with cans of cola, root beer and grape soda, a large bottle of water, a bottle of milk, a couple of bottles of wine (left from the last visitor). Of course, there were jams, jellies, and condiments of every kind.

There was little chance I would die of thirst, or bring me a hot dog and I was fully prepared.

The freezer was replete with frozen foods and half-gallon containers of butter-pecan ice cream. The last was so that the hot fudge would never be lonely.

Standing there, I felt myself becoming almost overwhelmed with the urge to clean out the refrigerator.

An alarm went off in my head. I know I'm procrastinating when cleaning the refrigerator seems like a good idea.

Grasping a thread of self-discipline, I chose instead to pour myself a glass of milk. That would hold me while I pulled myself away from the refrigerator.

I needn't worry, because the phone rang. It was Needy Danielle.

Wearing "needy pink" is optional for those who know the exact moment to make my phone ring to share their most urgent needs. Needy Danielles are irritating because they want you to do all of their thinking for them, but they don't listen to what you say when you do.

Needy Danielle's conversation was a really good example of the problem.

"I need to talk to you. You know, this afternoon when I took my nap. I've told you about my Sunday naps. Haven't I? They're delicious. Anyway, this afternoon while I was sleeping, I had the dream about a very sweet, and very handsome guy."

"Sounds wonderful," I remarked, though it sounded much like so many other dreams Danielle had called to share with me. Why she felt a need to keep me tuned in to her dream life, I wasn't quite sure.

"So, I was at Millennium Park, when I met this really tall guy. He was walking a cool dog. That dog had the most interesting eyes. I think you were in the dream too," Needy Danielle told me. She gave me a detailed, blow-by-blow description of her dream.

That morning's feeling of déjà vu was returning. Danielle sounded like she was describing Larry and the dog. Lost in that thought, I missed most of what went on in her dream.

Could Danielle really have dreamed what had occurred in my head that morning, when I saw her by the Bean while I was with Larry and the dog in Millennium Park?

"It felt so real. Have you ever seen a tall, handsome guy like that with a dog around the park? I need to find that guy. Do you think he's dating anyone?" she chirped.

I wanted to ask, "Whether who's dating anyone—the guy, or the dog with the interesting eyes?" But I said, "Danielle, it was a dream." She ignored me.

Needy D needed her dream to be true. "Do you think he needs a dog sitter? Did you think he was attracted to me? Should I get a haircut? What do you think the chances are that I would see him if I go to the park? Should I bring doggie treats for his pet?"

As you might guess I was able to think about my answers before I had a chance to actually give them. The answers? I kept them short and sweet.

"I don't know. No way to tell—guys are hard to read. Ask your stylist about the haircut. I have no clue how often he's at that park. Chances are 50-50. Doggie treats are a little forward. Don't you think?" She wasn't listening.

"Danielle," I continued. "It was a dream. It was all in your head!" but I was thinking about what was going on in mine.

Having completed the needy-questions protocol, we now could settle into a real conversation, but we already had used up over an hour. So I led the topic to my procrastination about looking at the photos my brother had sent, and Danielle found that a reason to say good-bye.

I needed a glass of wine.

I pulled down a glass. I cleaned my glass—by hand. I dried my glass—by hand. I held my glass up to the light to make sure it was spotless. I wiped it again—by hand. I opened and poured the wine—by hand. I knew I was still cleverly finding ways to procrastinate.

People undervalue procrastination. It has upheld the cleanliness of my abode.

I wasn't sure why I was overtaken by this avoidance behavior. I knew that the box contained photos I had seen before. I would just be looking at them for different reasons. Maybe my brain was working overtime to find ways to distract myself. Maybe I was just waiting for something to happen. I looked out at the night sky.

Looking at the night sky always calms me. Things look different, usually better, when it's night. People get more emotional at night. The lighting at night often makes faces glow and hides the flaws.

I lit some candles and got out my magnifying glass. Buoyed with the idea that the night sky and the harbor were right outside my window, I figured I was ready. I sat at my desk. I lifted the box to my lap.

But instead of opening the box, I closed my eyes.

To be accurate, instead of opening the box, I prepared to take a mental walk around my living room. I didn't need to suit up. What I had on was perfect for hanging out. I donned my headphones and selected some music.

Almost immediately, I heard the familiar ringtone of the front desk downstairs.

Why was the front desk calling me? I had already picked up Friday's package that I'd forgotten. I didn't order any food for delivery.

"Hi!" I answered, with my cheerful tenant voice.

"This is Lee at the front desk. You have a visitor, a Mr. Larry and his dog."

What was Lee doing in my head?

"Ah," I said, trying not to communicate my surprise, " Thank you. Send them up."

"Ma'am? We don't allow pets in this building."

"Oh, Lee, I'm sorry. Could you do me a favor? Could you show Larry to the freight elevator, and let his dog follow him up? Don't worry about it. No one seems to be worried about the three cats that live on seven or the African gray parrot that lives next door. Could I speak to Larry for a moment, please?"

"Hello, this is Larry."

"What a nice surprise. Listen, would you give our friend, Lee, $20 when he shows you to the freight elevator to let the dog up? He seems to think that the condo board wouldn't understand that the dog is a person. I'll reimburse you when you arrive."

"Sure thing."

Whoa. I was engaging in bribery. Which commandment covered bribery? It was probably the one about lying or the one about stealing . . . I didn't have time to figure that out.

I had no time to pick out clothes, so I went for a no-brainer choice. I kept the jeans, traded the beefy white t-shirt for a purple cashmere sweater, and added double-thick hiker's socks—not that I ever went hiking. I just liked the socks. I began pulling on my sweater to greet a Duesenberg-owning Larry and his dog on their first visit to my home. . . . Well, the version in my head anyway.

While I changed, I thought through what was in my refrigerator. Not a natural hostess, I'd been caught off guard. I decided I could offer them some wine and cheese.

I prepared for the usual comments that came when I opened the refrigerator's door. I figured I would explain that I have the culinary sophistication of a five-year-old. The rebel in me suggested that I might try winding a yarn about once having been obsessed with food, and now keeping myself limited to nutritional drinks, fruits, and an occasional hot fudge sundae.

I was hopping forward, putting on my second sock, as I went to answer the door. Larry held the door as the dog entered. The dog offered me a gift bag that contained a chilled bottle of my favorite wine. I thanked him and complimented him on his choice.

I gave my guests the 19-second tour, making sure they knew where the facilities were located. I offered the dog water in a cereal bowl, part of my quite ordinary set of dinnerware, and saw that he had a comfortable place to rest. Then I offered Larry a glass of wine. He accepted.

I opened the refrigerator. He made no comment. I lost an opportunity to tell a good tale. That made me curious about what might be in his refrigerator, but couldn't think of a way to ask.

We chatted as I opened and poured the wine.

"I just had the strangest phone call from Needy Danielle. You remember her from this morning by the Bean? She told me about this weird dream she had. It sounded like you were in it."

"What would be strange about that?" he said, with a glint in his eye.

"But this was the real person Danielle who called, not the one in my head. It was spooky how she could have been describing you and the events at the Bean," I said.

"Well, you don't think your imagination just makes up things do you? Your imagination and your subconscious gather information from reality the same way your conscious mind does."

"Well actually, I hadn't thought of it at all. So you're saying I run in a parallel reality of sorts?" I said, as we took our glasses and a beautifully prepared plate of cheese, grapes, and bread into the living room to sit on the area rug near my desk. The dog had moved to a new comfortable space at the foot of my desk chair.

"You could think of it that way," Larry answered.

"Wait. You mean that people who meet you when I am running in my mind can dream about you after I leave my run behind?" I found the idea amazing and not just a little bit unusual. "How do they carry on the story, when I've stopped thinking about them?"

Larry demurred from explaining the laws of metaphysics and said, "Think of it this way . . . they continue to exist even if you're no longer thinking about them. A strong story longs to complete itself so to speak."

"Wouldn't that make me like a god to them? I mean it's starting to sound like that age-old question, 'What if I'm just part of your dream or you're just part of mine?' Could be scary if someone decided to wake up."

"Yeah, it could be, if that's how it worked, but it's not," Larry assured me. "You just happen to be adept at mentally running your way into things that could actually happen. So, when you leave your run, scenarios often continue to play out. The dog and I sometimes hang around to find out the rest of the story."

I felt like I was back at that place where his words made a kind of sense, but I didn't have the code book. There must be holes in his logic. On the other hand, this could explain why my brain is always so busy, and why I have a story to answer any question I'm asked. I'd have to think on this more later.

To change the subject, I asked him if the dog had a raincoat, specifically one in "needy pink." Larry answered with a no and asked why.

I explained the concept of "needy pink," how Needy Danielle had earned the nickname, and how she could be called such despite the fact that she never wore that color.

Then I told him about my apparent hallucination the night of the party. The dog raised his head and scowled at the phrase *needy pink doggie raincoat.*

"Don't worry," I said to the dog. "I couldn't imagine you in a 'needy pink' doggie raincoat. That was what convinced me that it wasn't you two." The dog, appeased, returned his head back to his paws.

I had a passing thought about how this was so much better than looking through the photos.

Larry looked from me to the box on the cedar chest back to me and back to the box again. "Can't keep putting it off," was all he said.

It was clear there would be no further interruptions or excuses. I could argue with myself, but not with this guy who had taken residence in my head less than 48 hours ago. The box of old photos would be opened. It was inevitable.

We rose from the area rug on which we'd been seated.

I took the box from the cedar chest. I set it on a small file cabinet. Larry pulled photos from the box and laid them out across the desk. About 70 photographs looked back at us when he was done. Some were school pictures. The way school pictures are taken—line up; sit down; smile; shoot; go—they don't tell much about anything. We set those aside in a pile. Some were group pictures. Some were pictures of my brothers and me. Some were pictures from dance recitals, Camp Fire Girls carnivals, and other events through time. Those photos were set aside as well.

"Judging by these photos, you spend a lot of time in costume, Alice," Larry said with a laugh. He pointed to a picture of me at about age ten that looked like I was Alice in Wonderland. I had no recollection of the dress or the event. But it seemed a precursor of life events to come.

I looked across all the photos on the desk. I was both intrigued and unsettled by what I saw. Here was this little girl who was open to the world in some photos and hiding behind her mother in others. It was hard to tell that they were the same child. In one picture, I saw a shy child. In the next, I saw a child about the same age, but her face was so open that unconditional love was the only way to describe it. I wondered who coaxed the shy little girl to show so much of herself one time and not the other.

I stopped when I saw fear in my three-year-old face where I stood on a chair, as some adult had posed me, holding an old, black telephone receiver.

I remembered that day. How could I remember that day? Someone must have told me about it. Still, the feelings were still so real.

The St. Patrick's Day Shamrock Princess costume was itchy. The telephone was so heavy. The chair was so high from the floor. What if I fall? I could see myself in the mirror over the desk. I could see that I was afraid. Why were they making me be afraid? Where was my dad?

Why didn't someone notice how scared I was? Proof was there in the photo, right there in my eyes.

Larry was looking at more animated photos. "Look," he said. "No wonder they called you Mushy. Look at how many pictures where you're hugging someone, touching or holding hands with someone. You liked people a lot when you were a child. Look at that one. You're absolutely convulsing with laughter. Now there's something I'll bet you don't do often these days."

He was right on all counts, but I was hardly listening. I was taken by a thoughtful look on my face in a picture of me in a dancing costume. I was about four. The face was so relaxed, easy to read. It was serious and thoughtful like the little girl in *Miracle on 34th Street*. The girl in that picture felt good about herself and curious about life.

Next to it was a picture at about age eight, showing three generations of cousins. In that photo, my eyes say, "Tell me where to be, I feel like I don't belong."

And after that one, there was the picture of me standing in front of my dad. It was one of many, many pictures of me with my dad, but the only one in this batch. Still, only one was needed. He's standing behind me, over me like the biggest oak tree. A seven-year-old me is leaning back against him knowing I'll never fall, because he's there. His hands are on my shoulders. My smile starts at my mouth and goes all the way up to his face.

He's where I learned about unconditional love.

＊＊   ＊＊   ＊＊

In college I talked a whole passel of friends into driving to my hometown on a Tuesday night for pizza at my dad's saloon— it was a slow study week and the tavern was only an hour and a half away. So we piled in our cars for a road trip. I didn't tell my dad we were coming. That was part of the fun. There was no worry that he would be there. The saloon was his work, his social life, his other family, his natural habitat.

But I did tell my friends to watch his face when I walked in the door. They weren't disappointed. His smile reached out to the whole room. His friends around the massive slate bar reflected his smile with their feelings for him. He had no questions about what we were doing showing up for pizza on a Tuesday night mid-semester. It was the natural order of the world that such things should occur.

As I walked behind the bar to give him a kiss, his buddies teased, "Here comes the boss." "Give her $200, Dad." I turned to them and said I don't need anything more than that smile. I gave him a kiss on the cheek and he gave me a twenty when he shook my hand. It was our own secret handshake.

We had 8 or 10 of the best pizzas and a few beers to wash them down that night. My friends asked my dad what they owed him. He made a big production of thinking and writing, and thinking and writing, and figuring and adding, and erasing and adding. Then he said, "Best I can figure, it comes to $1.50 even."

On the way back, my boyfriend said, "One day I want to be the guy who puts that smile on your face."

※ ※ ※

"But look at this one," Larry said, pulling me back to the there and then. To the unobservant, it was just a picture, but in that picture was the proof that I had learned to go running in my mind before I was ten. As much as my eyes seemed to be peering at the camera, they were definitely looking inward. Those eyes weren't giving any secrets away. My hair follicles were too tiny for anyone to tell whether they had been sharing any secrets of their own.

"So what do we know now?" Larry asked, sitting back down on the area rug with the dog. I joined them, choosing to be where I could pet the dog. The dog reciprocated by placing his head closer to me.

"I think I was more versatile, or maybe I was simply fickle. Either way, I was easier to read as a child," I admitted. "I wasn't so invested in hiding my self-consciousness. I hadn't found so many ways to deny it. Maybe the world seemed safer then."

"Or maybe you were braver," he said. "I see your heart wide open in so many photos."

"Do you think so?" I said softly, while moving the blinds to change our view.

We kept company for a while longer. Larry, and the dog, and I watched the boats in the harbor. We watched the harbor lights moving on the water. We noticed the planes headed toward the airport forming a line of tiny white lights over the lake.

I opened my eyes and ended our evening together. The box of photos was still in my lap as it was when I closed my eyes to avoid it. I lifted the lid and saw the picture of the little girl posing by the telephone. I told her not to worry. She would grow up and would take that big tree in the backyard with her wherever she goes. There was no reason to be afraid ever again.

Then I went to bed smiling a smile that reached through time to the branches of that oak tree and the earliest days of my childhood.

Chapter Seventeen

A Cool Change

I GOT UP FOR WORK BEFORE DAWN, as usual. I decided to visit my thoughts, watching the sunrise from my living room, rather than down by the lake. Still wearing the long, soft t-shirt I'd slept in, I sat at the desk. A playlist I had put together at the start of my mind-running career sparkled back at me. It was a collection I had chosen for relighting my fires and tending my bruises. I had named this mix *Don't You Love the Sound?* after the Mark Knopfler song, "The Last Laugh," but the list opened with a Little River Band song called "Cool Change."

I sat back, closed my eyes and let the song carry me out to the sky.

> *If there's one thing in my life that's missing*
> *It's the time I spend alone*
> *Sailing on the cool and bright clear water . . .* [2]

Now that I had finally learned to empty my mind, I let the song carry me through the pre-dawn darkness, much like Peter Pan and the three Darlings as they flew off to Neverland the night they met.

I don't know how many songs went by after that first one. Possibly I had gone to Neverland, lived the story, and returned home before I heard the music again. I hadn't kept track. I no longer needed to record such things. I had learned to be secure in knowing when something was worth remembering.

Then I heard Larry's voice say, "So what do we know now?"

I almost answered out loud. Then I realized that I was alone in my head, remembering his question from last night. I was surprised Larry and the dog hadn't joined me, as had been their habit since that first time. For a small second, I worried that my new friends had abandoned me. I shook the paranoia from my head and went back to the sky.

As I waited for the sun, I considered my answer to Larry's question about what we know now. It had been something about being easier to read as a child and not so invested in hiding my self-consciousness. I had suggested that the world might have seemed safer. Larry had suggested that I might have been braver.

My answer wasn't nearly so telling as my approach to it. We had spent the whole night looking at pictures of a little girl and talking about her feelings. Yet when he asked me about what I knew, I responded with a thinker's—not a feeler's— answer. I wondered whether Larry had noticed it.

Or was that what he had meant when he said that maybe I was braver as a child?

Was I braver as a child?

THAT was something to think about.

I had been running through the stories I tell myself for three or four months now. I started when my boss started to find fault with me. Being at work had gotten progressively worse. My boss was watching my every move. Now he was encouraging my team and coworkers to find fault with me too. He regularly met with people I had considered as friends to say, "I know I'm the President, but don't be afraid to talk to me about every little thing your manager has done wrong." And enticed by the special attention he offered, many of them did.

⋟⋞ ⋟⋞ ⋟⋞

When I first started working for Benny, it was the best job, the coolest situation. My job description was perfectly tailored to who I am. The department I would manage had unraveled under the previous manager. The team walked around as if they had been whacked.

Benny treated me as the Golden Child. The one to re-teach the team their roles and the contribution they could make. I was the gentle force to bring back a safe environment in which they could be proud of their jobs. And it all worked well, until it wasn't working well at all.

Somewhere about year three or four, the team was back to brilliant. The Board of Directors started to question who was the outstanding leader that had brought the once weakest team to become such a success. The Board wanted to know more about me. They wanted to know how we had fixed what was broken, but unfortunately they gave all the credit to me.

I hadn't tried to attract that kind of attention. I had tried to keep a low profile, but the die was cast. Benny started to worry that he was losing stature in the eyes of the Board. In Benny's eyes, I went from Golden Child to threat.

⊰⊱ ⊰⊱ ⊰⊱

The problem with being the Golden Child is that people put you on a pedestal. That can feel so good, but it's not real and it doesn't last. When you let people put you on a pedestal you let them define who you are. To feel safe, they look to make you predictable by discussing your best characteristics. Now the definition is expanded to include their expectations of you.

And you never know what that definition is. Sooner or later you do something outside of that definition. It's something totally true to who you are. You exhibit a trait you never tried to hide. So you don't even know that you've stepped outside their definition of you. Though you had no evil intent or even awareness of their expectations, the people who put you on that pedestal interpret that misstep as a betrayal. And for that, they will want to punish you.

My halo had been replaced with horns.

My boss was watching my every move. He was encouraging people to find things wrong with my performance. I couldn't believe that it was happening. It happened so often that I had started running in my mind to find myself each morning before he pulled me apart each day at work.

I had been told to focus on work, not the people. I had done that so severely that work was all I was. I had edited nearly all of my friendships. I had been ordered to keep to myself, not to socialize with my team and coworkers.

My untenable position was the reason I had been thinking about thinking about things people do to think about nothing, and making rules to get some balance in my life.

As the sky started growing lighter, I remembered the talk Larry and I had about the little girl in the pictures. Out there in colors of the sky, something seemed to connect that little girl to the me who was going to work today. She was a wild child who found a way to blend every one of the 64 crayons into that sky. It was happening before my eyes. With blues turning into pinks, oranges, and yellows, the connection to that little girl magnified my heart in a deeply human way. I didn't have words for it yet, but I was beginning to get knowledge of what I had been missing. Sitting in the colors of the Monday morning sky, I felt my humanity beating and rising with the sun.

Then a computer alert interrupted what was happening.

My eyes flew open. Off went the music, off went the headphones, off went the long, soft t-shirt. If I didn't get my butt in gear, I would be late for work.

I transitioned in and out of the shower in record time—well, record time for me. On went the cream colored t-shirt, on went the walnut green long dress, on went the tan silk jacket and some off-white sport socks and canvas sneakers. Up went the hair. On went the makeup. So far so good.

In went the coffee and a breakfast bar and the morning migraine meds I'd forgotten to take earlier. A random thought of *here she comes and she's off her meds again* made me laugh out loud—though I supposed it was one of those things that only I would find funny these days. Probably not a good thing to share with people who already find you disturbingly unpredictable.

I did a pre-flight check. Had my glasses, check. Had my wallet, check. Had my keys, check. I grabbed my case and headed out the door. I'd like to say that the elevator was there waiting for me, but our elevators don't work like that. They wait at the lobby.

I pressed the button. It was there quickly enough. I had learned to time my departure at 6:45 precisely to avoid Mini-Cooper girl and again I was successful. The day was going my way.

My toy car, an MR2 Spyder—it wasn't really a toy, but with only 1.9 cubic feet of storage space, it wasn't really a grown-up's car either—was there waiting, but the 5'2" garage man, Nico, had parked it. It was about 6 inches away from a cinderblock wall. Getting in was going to be a trick. I had to get in sideways through a partially opened door. From there I had to push the seat back before I felt a glimmer of hope that I would get my legs in. It was a tight squeeze, but after a few adjustments I was ready to drive.

I started it up and headed out of the building. I took a right out of the driveway and looked into the last of the sunrise that had so affected me. I sat a little longer at the stop sign, letting traffic on the drive think I was a timid driver, while I enjoyed the view. Then I released my eyes from the sky and my foot from the brake, put the car in gear, and turned right again to pass the front of my building. At the next corner a third right took me to the next street where a fourth right was followed by a quick left. From there I headed west for the fourteen-block ride to work.

On a day like this one, many folks would have chosen to walk. I knew that. I just couldn't do that. I had been part of the sunrise that morning, now it was time to go to work. I could hear approximately 1.5 songs from my garage to where I parked my car.

During that time, I saw the city wake up. I saw guys get out of taxis and get into their cars at the local bar. I saw women and men walking their dogs. I saw people driving to work, stopping at the convenience store, walking down the street talking on phones.

Who did people call at 6:50 in the morning? It must be love.

At the 14th block, I took the fifth and final right turn. At the end of the block, just before the bus stop, I parked my car in front of the door to the office. Rockstar parking, everyone called it. It was fun. I could see my car from my office window. I unpacked myself from my little car and let myself into the building.

I dumped my bag in my office, logged on to my computer and opened the blinds. Then I went to the kitchen and started the coffee and while the coffee was becoming coffee, I stopped by Kai's office, a coworker who got to work while it was still dark, to see whether we needed to adjust the strategy on a launch our teams were producing together.

Kai peeked out from a pile of paper she was studying and pulled over her planner. Checking a rolling list she kept under my name, she mentioned two questions that needed quick decisions. After thinking for a minute, I made and communicated the decisions she required. Then she said she'd rather let the rest wait until later—she had to finish the document she was working on before an 8:00 meeting.

I headed back to the kitchen to get a cup of that coffee I had started earlier. Craig was there, pouring one for himself.

"Hiya!" I said, trying to start Monday with a charge of positive energy.

"How was your weekend?" Craig asked with more than a Monday morning sparkle in his eyes. "Did you enjoy the party? Anyone ask you to dance?"

"Ah yeah, I danced," I answered calmly. "But I think you already know. What did Des tell you about the party?"

"Des said that you two got the whole room dirty dancing! It sounded like you two made some real fun. He credits you at being a real pro at verbal volleyball. He said it's been a long time since he enjoyed a conversation so much."

"Yeah, he's a really good guy. I sure understand why you two are friends. I enjoyed meeting him. And you know, he just might be a better dancer than you," I teased. Luckily I hadn't poured my coffee yet, because Craig set his down and grabbed my hand. Next thing I knew we were doing the tango while he sang some unrecognizable tango sort of song.

When he spun me out, I let go, uncomfortable to be dancing at work. These days anything I did could be construed as inappropriate. Dancing seemed like a sure thing. When Craig reached for his coffee, I moved in a little closer to let him know I was serious. "You know, Craig, I really appreciate that you care enough to ensure that I had a good time. But Des said you suggested he come in your place a week ago. You really should have told me. I felt sort of weird when he said you told him there was dinner at the Hancock in it for him."

"He what? I didn't promise him dinner! That's his twisted sense of humor. He must have seen you were shook by finding out that I sent him. That would be his way of rattling your cage," Craig explained.

Craig's explanation helped. But then, in a way that only Craig could, he said just a little too much at the wrong time. "Anyway, I wish I could have been there. I know I would have had a good time. I sure enjoyed the chance to send Des. It was the next best thing to being there."

"Next best thing to being where?" Benny said, as he walked in behind us.

Craig and I exchanged glances that said, *This can't possibly turn out well.*

Craig came clean to Benny. "An actor friend, in town to make a movie, wanted something to do on the weekend. I suggested he join Alice at Richard's "Going Away to *NOT* Join the Army" Party. It sounds like they had a great time.

I didn't wait to get coffee. I headed to my office to check my email. A message from Benny, marked URGENT, demanded my response to an idea he had emailed to me late last night (while I was talking to Larry).

Wait. *He* told me no work this weekend.

No work this weekend had been an order. The lecture that went with it still stung. Working too hard was causing me to be unpredictable and abrupt. The younger members of my team didn't feel supported.

I found and read the email. He didn't want a response to his idea. Certain that his idea was good because he had it, he wanted a process map—a complete breakout by department of how the work that turned his idea into reality would flow through the company.

That no-work order was some sort of one-way work highway. I could think about new work he was making, but not the current work that needed to get done.

My reply, slightly more professional than what I was thinking, stated that I had received his message and I was starting on the process map at that very moment. And so I did, start the map that is. I had a meeting set with Benny at 10:30. I wanted to have at least the big picture view of the process ready by then.

I also was hoping to leave a little early today. A friend from college, Lucas, was in town for business. We were going to meet for business. Lucas and I communicated often, but I hadn't seen him for close to 20 years. Our workday ended at 4:00. Leaving around 3:30 usually wasn't a problem, especially since I got in at dawn.

The day passed quickly, as most days do. People were in and out of my office with things to look at, pages needing edits, and project problems to solve.

My boss stopped by at 10:15. Benny must have found out I had plans I cared about. He said, "Our 10:30 meeting won't work. But don't worry, I'll catch you later."

The process map, which had progressed fairly well for the first hour—the hour before the office opened—had hardly moved since. It was still in great shape by the 10:30 meeting that never happened. I worked on it for another half hour.

We had a senior-level status meeting at 11:00 that lasted until noon. At lunch, Benny's boss came to me with a request, saying a very old friend—*old* being the operative word here—was coming for lunch. He asked if I would mind moving my car, so that the friend, who had trouble walking, could park close to the front door. I eased his concern over inconveniencing me by saying that I had to take something home anyway. I did. I had decided to take my car home and grab a taxi back. It made more sense for Lucas to give me a ride home on his way out of town.

When I got back to the office 15 minutes later, I got a solid chance to move the process map further forward. I was feeling pretty good about where it was going. The sense of accomplishment felt good.

I was still working on it, when my boss looked in to announce, "I'm still planning to meet, but still can't say when."

I floated a better option, "I'm happy to put it off until tomorrow."

"No, no," he said. "I'll make it by to meet with you."

I was being held hostage . . . again.

At about 3:00, I finished the process map. At about 3:10 my phone rang. It was Lucas. His meeting in the suburbs had ended early and successfully. He'd be in the city earlier than expected. I gave him directions to the restaurant on the corner. I told him I was waiting on a meeting and apologized that he might have to wait. I was incredibly disappointed because I had said I would be able to leave early.

At 3:30, Benny sat down in my office. He let me show him the process map, but it was clearly an effort to follow form. He had no interest in the process map. He wanted to tell me that in the status meeting, I had been too polite, that I should speak up more. He said that one of my colleagues had complained that she thought I was withholding information.

This seemed strange. I'm rarely accused of not telling enough. After that same meeting last week, his feedback had been that I had gone too far into detail about the status of a big project.

I wondered at how, all of the sudden, my boss had become the telephone for everyone who had something to tell me. I wondered why he wasn't encouraging them to "dial direct," which was one of his mantras. At that very moment, he said, "Well, I think you need to talk it out together. We are in the communication business after all."

He did another litany on things that made me unpredictable.

The time I get my coffee changes? Seriously?

It became clear that our 10:30 meeting was put off to the end of the day early on. I doubted that my boss saw the irony in his behavior—how constantly changing the time we would meet was, well, the same unpredictable behavior he had accused me of. I knew it unwise to point that out.

However, I did take note of a shifting pattern. Last week, even in the email last night, I was a person and treated like one. Today, for some reason I was less than a person again. I had been demoted to the title of worker. This person, non-person, thing had been going on since he had told me that I should find balance in my life.

Today's balance was waiting at the restaurant down the street. Luckily, Lucas is a writer and natural people watcher. I could take some solace that he would be entertained by the humanity that passed by and through the restaurant. He was probably on a first-name basis with most of the staff by now. Hopefully, they hadn't invited him home to meet the kids.

My thoughts of my friend were interrupted by my boss's critique of my faults. I am tall and people find that intimidating.

Now this was getting personal. Was he about to suggest surgery?

I had worked for this company for years and no one had mentioned a problem with my height until today. Usually remarks about my height were comments on how I stay so slim or how I had the luck of a great gene pool. Always, they came from women.

Now a 6'5" man was lecturing me sternly on how tall people can be intimidating? He was telling me I needed to soften my style.

What effect did he think this not-at-all-soft conversation was having on the very-much-shorter-than-he-is little old me?

The clock said it was 4:45.

I was lost in a mire of mixed messages. I was sitting there past closing hour, listening to my boss tell me what was personally wrong with me, when I should be having dinner with a friend who is in town only for a few hours?

Last week this same boss said to quit staying late at work and get a life.

Forget about leaving early. Don't people who live a balanced life leave work on time to have dinner with a friend?

Where were all of these negative messages coming from? Benny was out there soliciting them. Did he realize that by carrying them back to me, he had ensured that the people sharing them had no reason to talk to me ever again?

I couldn't blame the folks giving him ammunition. It is a heady experience to have the big guy's ear, even bigger to have him slaying dragons for you. What kind of opera was being played out here?

The 64-color, beautiful sunrise had turned into this monochromatic verbal downer at sunset.

I opened my mind purposely letting Larry and the dog into my head so that I could once again communicate two things: "Grrrrrr!" and "You stay out of this." They knew that this time, the comments weren't meant for them.

That's when I heard it. Benny was on my case like a dad on a teenager—and he said, "I don't appreciate you and Craig undermining my request. I asked that you attend that party alone. You arranged for one of Craig's friends to take you instead. And you did that solely to circumvent my request." I just listened. In the end, my boss thanked me for taking the feedback so professionally.

My comeback—the one I should have said—surfaced as I was walking to the restaurant. It went something like this: "as opposed to the unprofessional way this meeting came to be, the unfeeling way the topics were covered, and the irony by which you actually do what you tell me not to do."

In editorial, we call that the inappropriate use of sarcasm to an authority figure and remind each other that it can get you nine to life.

I finally made it to meet Lucas at about 5:00. He was on his fifth cup of coffee. By then, he knew the history of the restaurant and the story of how it got its name. The picture of patience and politeness, he greeted me with "It's not fair, you look exactly the same."

To which I replied, "Nah, I look a whole lot better."

We talked about who we were and told each other our personal recollections of how we had met. It was an artful conversation of randomly weaving tales of the past with news of the present and ideas about what we should do. We asked questions that we never asked when we were both seventeen and explored the answers with the perspective of a life lived much longer. We explained ourselves as human beings and shared some of the impact we had had on each other's personality.

I threw in some of the frustration of my day. But publishing, like any soap opera, is hard to follow if you don't watch it every day. Lucas gave me words of wisdom based on his acute observation of the human species and his deep understanding of this person he knew so well. His words reminded me of who I had been, who I still was. He told me in narrative the story of the only time he had met my dad and what he saw that my dad saw in me. With the knack of a fabulous friend, never once did anything he say sound like advice or counsel.

At about 7:30 or 8:00, he drove me back to my building. He still had several hours of driving ahead before he found home. We said our good-byes, knowing that this time we'd keep the connection open. We were old enough now to know the value of a friendship that changes your life.

I rode up the elevator thinking of the sunrise that started the day and grateful for the conversation that ended it on a similar note. I set down my bag and went to my desk to look at the photos again. I spread them across my desk the same way Larry had.

I took my time remembering what I could about the photos, remembering the child I had been in each. I looked at the Alice picture, the curious dancer, the child who had learned to look inward while staring at the camera, and the fearful Shamrock Princess on the telephone, and told them all . . .

"If I grow up, I want to be just like all of you." I could feel their strength through and through me.

And I put on "Cool Change" one more time.

> *Now that my life is so pre-arranged*
> *I know that it's time for a cool change.*[3]

A change was happening. I had started running to find something else to fill the void—beginning to remember what else I used to think about besides work.

I'd spent weeks, months, trying to think of new things to think about with only minor success—the farthest I'd gotten with thinking about was building playlists. The reality was I needed to change my thinking altogether. Too much thinking was the problem, not what I was thinking about.

Ever since Larry and that dog had shown up, I had hardly had any chance to think. Everything had been about feelings. I'd had feelings. I'd gone completely out of character and acted upon them. I had shared my feelings and survived with little more than an anxiety hangover. And Larry and the dog were still talking to me.

How had I lost sight of my feelings? What had I done with them over all of these years? No wonder I seemed to be lacking balance. Where do I go to get my feelings back?

I sat back, put on the music, and closed my eyes.

In my mind I reimagined the photos on my desk. My feelings were there. I was seeing my feelings right there in the photos—in three little girls' eyes—my eyes.

I stared at the photos and tried to picture my own eyes as they looked at the pictures. What were my I eyes saying right now?

"They're saying that you want something very badly," Larry answered, appearing out of nowhere. The dog made a quiet purring sound. It did. It sounded little like a supportive purr.

I looked up and there they were with me again. But this time my eyes didn't change when they took in my two friends.

"I need to change," I said. "I need people to see in my eyes."

"That would be a cool change," Larry answered. "They would understand you more if you would share what's inside your eyes." The dog gave me a long look of love and concern, as if to prove the premise really worked.

"Look in my eyes, Larry. Teach me how to show them," I asked my friend.

Then I placed my hands around the dog's face and kissed his nose gently and said, "And if you will—for you are the master—could you make sure that he does it quickly and well?"

I'd lost too much time hiding already.

Chapter Eighteen

So Much Sky

I HAD JUST ASKED LARRY to help me change what the world finds in my eyes. We set the stage for a deeply productive and hopefully profound conversation. We opened the blinds full-wide to the clear night sky. I put on a playlist for all of us to enjoy, starting with a song called "A Long Way to Go," by the 70s band, Skylark. I left my oak tree on the riverbank in my childhood backyard.

Though I was still at my desk, eyes closed, imagining me discussing my life with a guy and his dog. It felt like we were in my living room real time.

We couldn't be together in real time. Could we?

Tonight we weren't exactly running through my memories, or

were we? It seemed we were preparing to go with the conversation wherever we needed the conversation to go.

We uncorked a bottle of wine and chose our unassigned seats
in front of the lake. Larry took the Lucite and velvet rocking
chair. I wheeled my executive chair from behind my desk next
to the rocking chair.

The dog started out on the floor at our feet, between us and
the lake out the window, protecting us from any ideas we
might have of ending it all with a jump. The dog would stay or
be wherever he wanted to be as the night went on. That was
very much this make-it-clear canine's way.

For a short time, I left man and dog to their own devices.

As I listened to the music, I sailed the night sky, thinking
that I had come a long way. I had come face to face with how
important it was for me to rewire my head to my heart. *That*
was the balance I needed.

A visual of a top-heavy me falling over from the weight of
my head jumped to mind and brought a smile. Then my eyes
dimmed like a laptop switched to power saving mode as the
visual dissolved, and I returned to knowing that I had to get
out of my head.

Like anyone considering a major lifestyle change, I had the
self-doubt tailor-made to undercut the change—even if the
change is the only thing that will save the life.

People facing lifestyle change can find themselves drowning
in a sea of questions. What if I try and fail? What if I try and
succeed? What if I succeed and no one notices? Worse, what if

I succeed and find that I've lost what I had and gained nothing to replace it?

I didn't need to go out every night, but I could see that I wasn't the best example of what the child in the photos might have grown up to be socially. So much potential hidden deep inside the safety of my mind.

Yet, at the thought of trying out real life full on, I felt that familiar self-consciousness creeping up, surrounding me. If I wasn't careful, I'd get that feeling-full hitch in my voice the first time I tried to say something important to Larry.

That wouldn't be good. People get distracted by the hitch in my voice. They get so busy wondering what I'm feeling, they don't hear the message—they miss the message that brought those feelings to bear.

Larry interrupted my thoughts. "Don't talk until you know what you want to say. Don't give in to a need to fill silence with words."

"I know. I know. My brain knows. My mouth forgets. Sadly, my mouth remembers quickly—as soon as my foot is lodged firmly within it. I know it for sure when I open my mouth to change feet," I said, thinking I might change the subject.

"Angel, you'll never get to heaven if you tell a lie," was all Larry said. The dog offered a look saying he was right.

Then my resolve caved. "That was a crafty, high-level deflection. Wasn't it?" I confessed. "I agreed with your point, and then I changed the subject in one fell swoop."

"Why do you do that . . . make light of a serious conversation?" he asked.

"Call it comic relief," I said, staring at the sky. I was taking my time. For once I was considering why spurts of clever remarks jump from my mouth when someone is just trying to talk to me.

"It has to do with pressure, I think. No, not pressure, fear— fear that you won't believe me, fear that you won't think I'm sincere. Or worse, fear that I'll answer with such intensity that my feelings will knock you over. I get lost and lose track of my impact when people start looking at me, especially when they await a response."

The sweet-thinking lowercase 'd' dog edged just a teeny bit closer to my feet. It was an act of support. The wise animal might have thought I didn't notice, or maybe he knew I did. Either way it was true comfort from a four-legged friend.

"You know, since you were tiny, you've been worried about people looking at you," Larry said matter-of-factly. "That's why you hid when strangers were around. Bashful One, not everyone was trying to judge you. Some people were admiring a beautiful little girl," Larry said, clear as the moonlight on the water.

Talk about a thought that had never been given air time. Why wouldn't I have thought that—ever?

I found myself saying, "I didn't hide for fun. It was for protection."

"What was the danger?" Larry asked.

"I'm not sure. Expectations. People had expectations. I didn't understand the rules. Far too often, I was misunderstood and judged wrong. I never had the correct response." I stopped to think about what I was saying.

"It's like the photo of the Shamrock Princess. You dress up a child and take her picture. She's supposed to like it. But what if she doesn't? That's a problem. What if she's afraid? You tell her there's nothing to be afraid of. You're telling her that her response is wrong, her feelings are wrong. She is wrong." I'd never said that before, but what I said was true.

"It doesn't make her less afraid," I went on. "It makes her feel wrong for being afraid. But she's not the one who's wrong, is she?"

I was taken aback. I was seized by what I had just said. I voiced a judgment about other people's actions.

Judgments scare me. If I judge people, then I could hardly fault them for judging me.

And the judgment I voiced felt even worse, because I hadn't put together that the "she" I had been defending was me until after I had criticized other people. I felt guilt and shame compounding the anxiety of having shared my feelings.

"What information you can glean from a photograph!" I think I said that to take my mind off my confused and guilty feelings.

I looked for a way to re-explain what I was trying to say. Times like these were always a bad time for me. When people listened intently, as Larry did now, I needed to know I was understood. I needed feedback or I would go on re-explaining for hours.

I had to tread carefully at times like these. Some people would actually listen for hours and then complain that I talked too much.

I went to the desk and picked up the princess picture.

That's when Larry said, "Let's go for a walk." He took the photo from my hand and placed it back on the desk. Then he looked at the dog and said, "What do you think, dog? How about a walk?" Like any co-conspirator worth his salt, the dog went straight for the door.

"We're going for a walk in the middle of a conversation because?" I asked, totally distracted from the mix of nasty feelings I had been about to wallow in.

"Because you need airing out," Larry said with a smile. "And so do we. So do we." I did the only thing I could think to do. I socked him in the shoulder half like I meant it.

I hate it when other people know what I need before I do. Then again, I love it, too.

The rush of fresh air as we stepped into the night was spectacular. We weren't looking out at the sky. We were out in the sky. My feelings had a universe in which to expand and they seemed small in comparison to that space.

By some tacit agreement, we three headed in the same direction, to the most open spot in the front of the building. Larry and the dog let me walk a little ahead to get my bearings. The street was too bright to see stars under the city lights, but I didn't care. The space was amazing. I thought of Julia Macklin's song "So Much Sky:"

> *Had enough of answers,*
> *answers bore me*
> *when there's so much sky*[4]

I slowed to rejoin my pals.

Yeah, *my pals*, I like that. I think.

We turned down the side street of historical houses and grand old trees. It's a fine street for walking and talking, romantic and roomy. Low stone walls, most graced with wrought iron fencing, have lined the sidewalks since the 1890s. The walls were perfect for sitting to talk long into the night under old, stately trees which seemed strategically placed to protect confidences you might share.

We chose one of those stone walls in front of an old house, under stately trees. We sat where we could admire the houses across the street. The ambiance was almost like being in another city, one without tall buildings or traffic. It was something like being three eccentric characters in modern-day dress on a set for a beautiful 19th century period drama.

"You know," Larry said, "every kid has probably been in the situation of that princess picture. Why does it rile you so?"

"It's the helplessness. It's the lack of respect. It's that everyone forgot that the child was a person. The situation was scary. The child couldn't have known what was happening, and she was totally helpless to stop it. She doesn't like it. She was saying so with her eyes."

"The people who took that picture didn't notice," Larry said. The caramel-eyed dog made a slight whimper of agreement. His caramel eyes seemed to lose some brightness. He laid his head down as if his eyes had been made tired by the thought of the picture-taking event.

"And they didn't help her," I repeated quietly. "That's why it riles me. It seems as if they made her helpless, and then no one chose to help her."

We leaned back against the wrought iron fence that was part of the stone wall on which we sat and looked up through the leaves at the night sky. The backlit leaves made it hard to hold a grudge against any human's failings . . . even my own. There was more than enough room for mistakes on a planet that held such beauty and so much life.

A noise drew my attention and a small, spring bunny showed itself under an azalea bush just beyond the fence. It was the joy of playing in the bark mulch without having to get my hands dirty. I guess there was a genuine upside to not thinking so much.

"So are you ready to go drink more wine and tackle more answers?" Larry asked.

"Nah, I've had enough of answers for one night," I said. "You guys head on home. I think I'll go for a walk by the lake. Who needs answers when there's so much sky?" I said, as I silently thanked Julia Macklin for reminding me about where my priorities should lie.

And so I headed off toward the lake to commune with the sky . . . and the dog followed behind me. I don't think he liked the idea of me walking the lakefront alone at night.

Chapter Nineteen

I Keep Dancing

THE DOG AND I WALKED out to the lake and wandered a while until we found a spot with an exceptional view. Then we sat ourselves down, me with my arms around my knees and he with his head against my knees. Next thing you know, I was scratching his head, which I think, was part of his evil plot to bring me out of my thoughts.

Eventually I laid my head on his. It was nice bonding with the dog. I was beginning to understand why Larry was hesitant to choose a name for this dog—a dog who certainly was his own dog. I still smile to think of sharing that moment with the only dog I think of as more than a friend. Still in my head, it was around 2 a.m. when the dog walked me back to my building, as any Gentledog would.

Ending that story, I opened my eyes. I stayed at my desk to stack the photos spread across it into a pile. I figured that I had done enough obsessing in that direction for a while. Feeling calmer, I left my desk and headed back to my bedroom for some sleep.

No indecisiveness in front of the closet tonight. Last night's decision had set the week. It took seconds to pick out the red long dress and the teddy bear shirt to wear to work in the morning. Then I found the way to my pillow. My brain was free of things to think about. It was filled with sky. Sleep came without work or worry.

The morning came early, but I didn't mind. I had plenty of time for myself before I needed to leave for work. I started the coffee, went to my desk, and turned on my computer to read my daily horoscope. It said I was going through a time of change and that I should let go of the things of the past in order to take advantage of what the future had to offer. I wondered how many people would find those same words. I went to get a cup of that coffee.

Feeling relaxed and rebellious, I couldn't wait to watch the sunrise. I called down to the garage to say that I'd be picking up my car about 20 minutes later than usual. Then I headed for the routine transitions of the morning: shower, clothes, make-up, hair, and mindset. I returned to my desk chair to await the first glimmer of color in the sky.

I put my entire music collection on shuffle and closed my eyes.

I reached for the stack of photos, I did a random choosing of one from the middle of the deck. The song that came on was one by Norah Jones called "Seven Years." The song made me see the singer as a little girl full of life, dancing, laughing, turning and twirling.

The photo I had pulled was the picture of the curious dancer. The young dancer, me, looked so secure in front of the camera, she of *Miracle on 34th Street* child-star look. I spent a few minutes thinking of the time I had spent dancing as a child. I glanced up at the Hillel quote framed on my bookshelf that said, "I get up. I walk. I fall down. Meanwhile, I keep dancing."

I thought about how dancing had been part of my life since I was three-and-a-half years old. My mother once told me she gave me dance lessons because she thought I was clumsy and needed some grace. I knew I could be wrong about that, because I'd often repeated such rememberings years later to my mother or my aunt only to hear them swear that they never said such things.

My cousins have had similar experiences of remembering things that my mom and my aunt have sworn they haven't said. Go figure.

I stopped my thoughts to see whether the loudspeaker from heaven would bring an announcement from my mom to set me straight, but it appeared she was going to let this small fish go.

Dancing had become such a part of my life so early, it was like walking for me. I didn't think about it. Nor did I think about how much time I spent doing it.

One day when I was in college, my cousin Katerina said, "Oh, no point in asking you to play, when you were a kid. You were always in the basement wearing your dancing shoes."

Little did she or anyone else know that I hadn't stopped dancing. Even today when I was waiting in an elevator or a hallway alone, I often did a dance step and wondered whether I was on some security tape somewhere looking ridiculous doing it. Sometimes I danced down a sidewalk when no one was looking. And of course, I often danced in my head, which goes without saying.

I looked down again and stared at the photo of the curious and open dancer. No wonder she wasn't self-conscious. She had learned to dance when no one was looking, while it was safe, a little bit at a time. She was a part of me I should hold on to. I liked her. She was curious and open and strong.

Setting down the photo, I noticed that the first glimmer of light was breaking the horizon. Then I decided to go outside to watch the sunrise.

With that thought, I opened my eyes and turned the music off.

I gathered my things for work, got myself outside, and I positioned myself on a bench in the grassy area between my building and the next. I was well away from the foot traffic with a head-on view of the lake and the sky, and in the privacy of a space not often used.

Watching a sunrise is like watching God's version of what stop-motion video should be—the ultimate grown-up kaleidoscope. The colors move and change, blending and curving and curling, making and faking giant patterns. Your eyes cannot see the movement happening, only the results. It's intimidating and invigorating at the same time. It's a magic show of light that can be explained by science but not quite reproduced.

An exact photograph, a perfect painting of what I saw that morning would look unreal—like it couldn't have happened—because a sunrise is not meant to be flat and tangible. It is meant by nature to be fluid and ethereal. That's why a real sunrise fills me up in a way a photograph can only remind me.

I enjoyed this particular sunrise long after it was over. I let every part of me enjoy the luxury of time that had gone into that sunrise. Nothing had hurried the sunrise. No one had tried to make it happen faster. The sunrise took exactly as many minutes as it needed and not one minute more. It was a perfect sunrise just as it was. That's when I realized that I had no reason to hurry either. No work called me to arrive at my office by 6:45, and the bench felt like a fine place to spend my time.

A conversation I had with a twenty-something friend returned to me. It had been about relaxing and letting people see who she really is. It had started because she had felt she had made a mistake, but soon got to the real problem.

❧ ❧ ❧

"The world doesn't feel very safe to me. People don't take me seriously. People who I used to think were my friends now act like I'm some sort of doofus. They're always ready to look for what's wrong with me," my friend had revealed when no one was looking.

"I know about that. People like you and me often make that happen. We use self-deprecating humor so that people don't look at us too closely. We entertain them and they enjoy that—for a while. But it's wearing and takes patience to deal with someone who's always in entertainment mode."

"Yeah," she said. "But they know my work."

"Sure they do. But they want to know they can trust your work" I answered. "The people worth knowing want to know who you are. They know that they're not getting the whole story. The people you mention don't need friends for entertainment," I had said.

"But I'm not hiding anything. I wouldn't hurt anyone," my friend had replied.

"Well, yes and no," I answered. "You're not hiding anything. Still, I'll bet that hardly anyone knows that you speak three languages and you play three instruments. Why not relax a little and let them know who you are? Then your self-deprecating humor will have context and heart. People will respect you and laugh with you.

"Also know this," I went on. "You may never mean to hurt someone, but all of us can."

My younger friend had tried what I had suggested and it had worked for her. She became a respected member of her group. Her opinion mattered. She was no longer what she had called the doofus—someone who was suspected and frowned upon.

⋇   ⋇   ⋇

I wondered why I didn't listen to my own advice? I closed my eyes and heard Larry's voice say, "It's about time you asked yourself that question."

I was getting used to these bizarre appearances by now. It didn't even phase me when I heard a yip punctuate Larry's sentence. I opened my eyes.

Why didn't I relax and let people know who I am?

Finished with my sunrise thinking out on the bench, I went inside to get my car and got myself to work.

Work was uncharacteristically uneventful. Benny was out of town and the progress on most of my projects was going as planned. In fact, as days go, it bordered on boring. I like a problem to solve now and then. On the other hand, it was nice to know that I was able to be a person again without worry of reprisal.

At 4:00, I headed home, parked my car and went upstairs.

I entered my condo and went to my desk. I had to think about things. Maybe Larry could help.

I put on my headphones, started some music and closed my eyes.

I thought I heard my phone ring. It was Larry. I knew it was Larry because my phone said so. Actually it said, "Larry & dog." I answered it.

"You made my phone ring," I said.

"Why, yes, I did," he stated factually.

"My phone knew it was you," I replied in the same manner.

"Is that something special?" he asked quite clinically.

"Yes it is, since I don't have your number," I answered.

"It's magic, I guess," he said without missing a beat.

"You're not going to explain, are you?" I stated without hope.

"Correct again. Right now, I'm not," Larry answered.

"Ah, so there is hope for a future answer?" I pushed.

"Only if we can move on to other things now," Larry warned.

"So, how may I help you?" I asked.

"I thought you might like to go to dinner," he invited.

"Tonight?"

"Yes, tonight," he said calmly.

"With you?

"Yes, with me." He was starting to sound a teeny bit impatient.

"But I don't know of any restaurants that allow dogs."

"That's quite all right," Larry replied. "He's not coming."

Chapter Twenty

A Packard and a Teddy Bear Shirt

I HAD JUST DISCONNECTED the call when Larry called back.

"Yes, sir," I said.

"I'm bringing the Packard. It's a convertible. So you might want to bring a jacket. I'll be by around 5:30. Can you be ready by then?"

"Where are we going?" I asked.

"To dinner, like I said," Larry answered.

"Anything special I should wear?"

"Anything you might wear to an underground war bunker."

"A what?"

"I forgot. It's been a while since you've been there. It's been a while since you had any fun at all."

"Hey, I had fun once."

"Try for some jeans, a cotton shirt, maybe a babushka and a denim jacket, if you have one," he advised.

"I have one. Why isn't the dog coming?"

"He's made other plans. Gotta go," Larry said and hung up.

I had to give him credit. He had my attention.

Without removing my headphones, stopping the music, or leaving my mind, I checked the clock on my phone and got ready. It was 4:45. I had time. I did the shower thing, the make-up thing, the jeans-and-cotton-shirt thing—at least I didn't have to decide what to wear—and was ready to go by 5:00.

With a half hour to spare, I turned my thoughts back into the music that was on shuffle. In my mind I opened a scrapbook my mom had left me. As I was paging through I saw a photograph of me in a certain alphabet shirt that had once been my favorite.

Next thing I knew I was transported through time again.

✦ ✦ ✦

I was about four. My dad, my dancing shoes, and the alphabet
were the only friends I needed. They kept me busy from
morning until night. If I wasn't with my dad, I was dancing.
If I wasn't dancing, I was writing my letters until they were
perfectly formed. I loved words, even then. I loved how they
looked. I loved how it felt to write them.

My grandmother thought my parents should take my letters,
my pencils, my paper, all of it away from me and instead
make me go outside to play like a "normal" child. But my
mother defended me and told everyone to mind their own
business. I was a happy child as I was.

My dad had a friend. I didn't even know the man's name.
He was a trucker who did odd jobs for my dad on the side.
At some time my dad must have told his friend that I was
obsessed with the alphabet, because one day my dad came
home with an ABC shirt for me that the trucker man had
picked up in Arizona. I thought it was cool, especially because
the postal abbreviation for Arizona was AZ.

About six months later my dad said that the trucker guy was
coming over to clean the eaves on our house. I ran to my
room to put on that shirt. When the doorbell rang I ran to
open the door, my eyes were bright with "look what I did
to say thank you." The trucker guy didn't notice. He walked
right passed me.

✦ ✦ ✦

The sweet voice of Kasey Chambers came on in my headphones. The words asked the questions of a person who felt invisible.

I thought about the song and my alphabet shirt story. It's not that I was drowning in self-pity. It was thoughts of a gift gone unanswered. The loss was as much the trucker's as my own . . . only he didn't know it. Meanwhile I had to adjust the picture in my head, change my paradigm. I've done a lot of paradigm shifting in my life.

I closed the scrapbook and picked up the picture of the curious dancer.

"What would you think of this whole thing?" I asked the picture, and thought about what she—the child I was—would have had to say. The answer didn't come to me in words, but in feelings. The feelings basically said, "Nobody is going to die and we're still going to dance tomorrow."

I thought that philosophy was as good as any. I looked at the picture again and wished the child a thought-filled thank you, reminding myself to keep this part of me alive and well. Then I set the photo back on my desk.

I was still considering her advice, *Nobody is going to die and we're still going to dance tomorrow,* when I received a text from Larry saying he was downstairs.

I thought an answer to his text and sent it. Then I grabbed my denim jacket. I skipped the elevator and and simply thought myself downstairs. Having gathered energy and achieved a "we're still going to dance tomorrow" philosophy, I was ready for whatever this night would hold. At least I hoped so.

I was wrong. At least about the car, that is. The car was ever so much more that I was ready for.

I walked out the revolving door and was dazzled by a vision that made the Doozy look like a second-choice ride. Here was a 1934 stunningly understated platinum silver Packard V12 Cabriolet Touring Car. I had to stare just to take in the beauty of the mirror finish and the sleek lines of this long, lustrous driving machine.

I couldn't resist. I took the prescribed babushka—really a lightweight cashmere scarf—from around my neck, wrapped it lightly around my hand, asked permission with my eyes, and got a nod. Then I thoroughly enjoyed the chance to slide my hand wrapped in cashmere along the rolling hills of the Packard—a beautifully sculptured work of art. Say what you will, but some things are better experienced second-hand than not at all.

Larry graciously opened the passenger door for me. I ran my hand over the seats, the dashboard, the carpet, the running boards. I felt like a little kid, seeing a car for the very first time. It was like being five years old and tasting chocolate pudding for the very first time. There are no words for how perfectly beautiful this car appealed to all of the senses, offering the precise amount of attention and not one iota more.

When I became at risk of drawing a crowd over my reaction, I begrudgingly took my seat in the car and prepared for a ride. I placed the scarf in correct babushka position to protect my hair from the inevitable bug-catching that occurs whenever hair moves through the air at speeds over 1 mile per hour. I noticed how quickly my mindset became "you are riding in a car, but I am riding in this glorious 1934 Packard V12 Cabriolet

Touring Car." I sat back in the comfort intended for people much richer than me from a time gone by. I wondered what it would take for someone to take such quality and comfort for granted, and said a little prayer that I would always be surprised by such things.

"That's a great shirt," Larry said, as he put on an old-fashioned driving cap and pulled out of the driveway to head north on the inner drive. I had decided that the teddy bear shirt still fit the bill for this dinner adventure we were taking in the Packard.

"Yeah, I'm wearing a teddy bear shirt, and you're not," I said, with a touch of little-girl pride and a very big smile.

"Well, I'm glad to see that you're not still mourning your ABC shirt," Larry said, with a wink.

"Stop that," I said. "I hate it when you do that."

"Do what?" He asked, the picture of innocence cruising along in a fabulous car.

"Tell me that you know things that you should have no way of knowing."

"But isn't that what you do that scares people all of the time?" he asked.

"I'm not sure I know what you mean," I said.

"When you look in their eyes and tell them what they are thinking. Isn't that the same thing—telling them things that you should have no way of knowing?"

Caught again. He was right, wasn't he? He had given me a taste of my own medicine. Is that what he had been doing all along? If that was what this was about . . . I didn't think I liked it. In fact I was sure I didn't like it at all.

"But let's get something straight," I said, with a charge of vehemence I was trying to keep under control. "I don't try to teach people a lesson, and I don't try to use what people are thinking against them; that would be just wrong. The most I try to do is make them aware of what they're doing."

"From your tone of voice, I get the feeling that you think I might be doing something other than that," Larry said, with a calmness that was irritating and unnerving at the same time.

"You're trying to teach me a lesson," I said, taking my corner. "You're sticking a pin in a place where I'm vulnerable, and twisting it around."

"I'm sorry you see it that way, but my intent was not to teach a lesson. I was just talking. If you're getting the feeling that there's a lesson here, you're finding it on your own. You've always been a quick study, you know." He gave me a few minutes to realize that I had been riding a wave of adrenaline to jump to a pretty large conclusion.

I got his point. "Wow, I'm a jerk. I'm sorry. Talk about someone who's got an issue."

"I'd be happy to do whatever I can to help remove that pin you've got sticking in you," he said, without hurt or judgment. "So that we can get on with enjoying our night out in the Packard."

"Oh, I think I've got that under control now," I said. "What if we just sit back and enjoy the ride for a mile or two?"

And that's just what we did until we had left the city lights behind us.

As soon as we were well on the back roads—for some reason I had the feeling we were taking a circuitous route to wherever we were going—Larry pulled out an iPhone and a set of speakers just for the occasion.

"Rumor has it that all of your friends are operations managers," he said.

"Well, some by trade, but most by personality," I laughed.

"I can't say as I qualify by either, but I figured it was important at least to give it a shot. So I thought you should have some appropriate music, and I needed you to be listening to me, so I couldn't let you do the choosing."

"I understand. Your car, your trip, your agenda, your music. Makes sense to me. Except . . . "

"Except what?"

"Except, where's the dog?"

"I'll get to that in a minute. Do you mind if I pull over? With these hands, I can't set this up the way I want it and drive at the same time."

As you might guess, the image of two bunches of bananas, one holding the wheel of a beautiful vintage car, and the other trying to set up the speakers to make the perfect sound experience while he held the iPhone tightly in his teeth, jumped into my mind. I began giggling, then laughing, and couldn't stop. He looked at me and then, as if he knew, he just shook his head, blushed, and went about the business of setting up the perfect sound experience.

Larry let me read the playlist as he worked. Every song on it had one of these words in the title: *moon, star, sky, sun.* I knew every one of them from sometime in my past. It started with "Rooty, Toot Toot for the Moon," the Michael Johnson version. I had listened to that song almost every day in college, and had gone to see Michael Johnson play (and collected a hug) with my friend Michele about three or four years ago. It had been like meeting an old friend after years of being apart.

Music ready, we listened to the first song as we got back on the road and got our bearings before we started talking.

Once again it seemed that God was in His heaven; angels were everywhere; and all was right with the world, my world anyway. Except, of course, I wished the dog were there.

I missed the lowercase 'd' dog a lot.

Chapter Twenty one

A Safe House

WHEN THE SONG WAS OVER Larry said, "What do you think about when you look at the sky?"

"I don't really think about anything. I just am. It's just me and the planet and the sky," I said. "I let go of thinking and let my mind become part of the sky, that's why I go running in my head to get away from my head—sounds kind of crazy, I suppose, but it works."

"Sounds a lot like what you say happens when you're with your friends, your lifelong friends," Larry put in.

"Yeah, it is. Good friends make a kind of music together. It's like harmony that requires no work."

"Where'd you learn to do that, be with friends like that?" he asked.

"That's easy, my dad. No question, my dad. He was like that tree in my backyard—always there, always ready for me to lean against him, hug him, whatever. He was a safe house for me. He was a special guy, my dad."

"He had a special daughter," Larry said.

"It's that gene pool thing." I said.

"No." Larry stopped me. "Don't make light. Haven't you ever thought about it?"

"Thought about what exactly?"

"Thought about how much you are your father's daughter? And your mother's."

"Well, actually, I have."

"Then it's beyond me why someone who was that curious dancer, who is the daughter of that father and that mother would be hiding herself in her head, like you are right now," Larry declared.

I didn't have an answer. I'm not even sure I understood the premise. Since he had mentioned her, I thought of the curious dancer. What would she say? Heck, she would probably ask him to dance—and he would probably pull over and do just that.

"Larry, do you dance?"

"I've been known to when the occasion calls for it. None of that dirty dancing in costume stuff, but some regular dancing, some romantic moonlight dancing and a little cowboy line dancing—Cotton-Eyed Joe in particular—when the spirit calls."

"I'd never guess that you'd have the boots for it," I smiled.

"Bull-shit!" he called in true Cotton-Eyed Joe style, and I knew he knew what he was talking about. Imagine that—a line dancing, Packard-driving, mind-running Larry. Even my imagination never would have gone there on its own.

"Why'd you ask?"

"Because I'm my father's daughter . . . and my mother's." That was the truth and I liked myself for saying it. I also liked myself for being it. I also liked myself for listening to the curious dancer in me. *Nobody's going to die, and we're still going to dance tomorrow.*

The Doobie Brothers song, "White Sun," came over the speakers that my banana-hand friend had jerry-rigged for entertainment. The song carried us along into the city of Milwaukee just as the sun was getting low on the horizon.

> *And I slip away down by the water*
> *And I slip away down by the sea*
> *Take love and give love*
> *It's got to be.[5]*

How could I not feel grand with the light, the sky, the music, the car, and the banana-hand, Cotton-Eyed-Joe dancing friend at my side?

We turned right to a part of town I didn't know, and Larry seemed to know exactly where he was going. He did. We pulled the car into a vintage car dealership that appeared to have stayed open waiting for us. A guy named Jack tossed Larry the keys to the place, and told him where to put them when we picked up the car later.

"Whoa, you have clout!" I said as we walked away from the building. "He gives you the keys to his shop."

"Nah, he doesn't want to have to wait for us," Larry answered. "He has a family at home—two little girls and a beautiful wife, who dote on him, and he doesn't want to miss a minute of their attentions, which, by the way, he returns a hundredfold."

"Your world sure is a wonderful place," I remarked.

"It's *your* world, silly," he corrected. "*You* made it happen. We're in *your head.*"

I stopped dead on the pavement and stood directly in his path. "One of these days, Mr. Larry whatever your name is, you're going to tell me what you mean when you say things like that," I said, looking straight into his blue eyes.

"Yep, you called that right, and tonight's the night. But let's eat first." And he jogged a little to get around me, grabbed my right hand in his and started walking again. We were headed in the direction of a block of what looked to be business buildings that were all closed for the day.

"Where are we going?" I asked.

"You keep asking, and I keep telling you . . . to dinner. Have a little faith in me. What kind of an aspiring angel can you be, if you can't have a little faith?" he smiled.

I slowly shook my head and soldiered on, wondering what he was up to, but now convinced that he knew exactly where he was going, and why.

We ended up in front of a plain red door set in between two unassuming outdoor sconces hanging off one of a row of plain stucco buildings. To one side of the door was a simple red and green awning. To the other side, under the sconce, was an unassuming plaque that said "International Exports." Larry tried the door and to my surprise, it opened. Inside the door was a small entryway. The only furniture was a 1940s plug-in-style telephone switchboard. No attendant was sitting there. No person was in sight. Nor did it appear that one had been since that switchboard had been practical to use.

"It appears we're in the wrong place," I said quietly, having a distinct chilling feeling and a heartfelt wish to back right out again.

"Wait," Larry whispered, as if he heard something.

Then a voice seemed to come from nowhere. I shook my head to make sure I heard it. I'm not sure what it said, but I heard Larry gave some sort of password. Then a door I hadn't recognized as a door opened. We walked downstairs and found ourselves in a safe house from World War II.

The place was amazing. The ceiling was low. The walls were made of sandbags. Many James Bond types, both male and female, with briefcases were gathered around a small bar at the foot of the stairs drinking exotic drinks and talking about old spy movies, among other things. I heard one guy call

himself a VIO and another debunk the idea by saying that the
first was a "Very Important Operative" in the same way that
Inspector Gadget was a very important inventor.

A video screen displayed any action at the switchboard—the
same switchboard where we had just stood. Apparently, those
attempting to enter without a password are interrogated, and
asked to prove their loyalty by entertaining the spies inside. I
thought a short thank you to Larry for doing his homework on
that issue.

Though I hadn't said my thank you aloud, Larry replied as
if I had. "What VIO wouldn't go to such extremes for a self-
conscious lady-friend?"

I responded to his remark by doing what my six cousins had
taught me to do at times like these—I socked him in the
shoulder like I half meant it.

As we walked farther into the place, Larry told me a bit about
what I was seeing . . .

"Should you wish to make a call to any of your lifelong friends,
use that telephone booth. It is equipped with a variety of
sound effects for background noises, such ambiance as a
bowling alley, a Russian submarine, or my favorite, bombs
going off. 'Hello, honey, can't get home right now. We're
having a real war at the office.'

"At that back bar Sneaky Pete gives patrons an education in
spying, magic, gambling, and other tricks of the trade. Watch
out for trick mirrors, especially in the women's washroom.
You'll probably find scanners in there as well. Also, we
won't be leaving the way we came in; the exit is through that
telephone booth over there.

"Our table is in the puzzle room. It's this way. The wall on the right is the puzzle." For a crowded space it was surprising, at first, to see how we went right to a table meant for us. Then I realized I was with Larry, Larry of Larry and the dog fame, Larry of the Doozy and the Packard fame, Larry who could interrupt my thoughts by becoming part of them—getting a table in a restaurant in Milwaukee should be a piece of cake in his world.

"Like I said, *your* world, *your* world," he corrected.

I wish I could stop being irritated by Larry's apparent mind-reading abilities. I was careful not to think about anything I wasn't absolutely positive I wanted Larry to know. But I had to admit, it was starting to become a comfort that he was listening to my thoughts. Even more than that, my curiosity had taken hold. I was dying to find out how he always seemed to hear my thoughts. I was going to hold him to that statement he made earlier . . . I was going to find out how he knew so much about me. I was going to find out tonight.

We sat and pulled our menus from a mechanical hand on an overhead track system that ran around the room to each table. It was like a toy train system, only better. When the track got to your table, the piece that was yours came down to you.

As we perused the menus, I considered my relationship with Larry. Much as I might wish otherwise, I knew my conversations with Larry only took place in my mind. Even so, we covered a lot of ground, and I still didn't know his last name. My dad wouldn't like that I went even one day without knowing his full name—not that he'd ever find fault with my choices.

"He'd make an exception in my case," Larry interjected.

"Stop that," I said slapping my menu lightly on the table— the table was too wide to give his shoulder a sock. I looked over at the moving puzzle on the wall to clear my thoughts. It was fascinating and somewhat mesmerizing. Then, when he didn't expect it, I looked back at Larry with my brow furrowed over a stern face and said, "Now what am I thinking?"

"You're thinking that I should stop listening in on what you're thinking, and that I need to see that face to know that you're not happy that I've been doing it in the first place," he laughed. "It's a waste of a good face, though, I already knew you didn't like it."

"But you did it anyway."

"Yes I did, because you think too much . . . and because I'd like to be part of the conversation. I invited you to dinner. You're my guest. It was the only way I could get your attention without embarrassing you. I didn't want to make you feel bad for leaving me out."

"I'm sorry. I'm back and you have my undivided attention." I reverted to a word game my friends used to play in college. "So now what do you want to talk about? I don't know. What do you want to talk about? I don't know. What do you want to talk about?"

Larry said, "Okay, I get your point. How about if I pose a non-threatening question? How do you think people get information about other people?"

Just then a mechanical hand came down with an order pad and a pencil. We filled in our orders, put them back in the hand, and sent the hand on its way.

"Oh no!" I feigned distress. "We forgot to wipe the hand for fingerprints, and oh dear, we didn't check for bugs," I said leaning closer to Larry and looking both ways out of the corners of my eyes.

"No worries," he said. "I have a mole in the kitchen. He'll take care of that. We're covered."

"Hope the mole's—two legs or four?—not cooking our dinner," I said.

"No diversions," Larry countered. "Back to the question—how do most people learn about other people?"

"That's a big question." I was stalling for time.

"We've got plenty of time." He knew I was stalling.

"All right, let me think this through so that I can do this in an organized fashion. I would guess that we could group people by the way they gather information. To simplify the argument, can we assume that everyone uses more than one way, and just talk about people's preferred way of getting information?"

"Hey, I was making conversation, not setting the premise for a research report," Larry said, in his own way telling me to quit with the disclaimers and get on with it.

"Let's start with the ones who don't do the work. They rely on other people's opinions at every turn. They read tabloids or listen to gossip. If stuck with deciding on a person that no one can give them information on, they make a decision based solely on a previous decision about a totally different person. The thinking goes something like this: *Noel always lies about what she does on the weekend and Jenny is her friend, so Jenny must lie about such things too."*

Larry said, "I've met a few of them. They do well in jobs where thinking is a not a requisite skill, but in fact a danger or a disruption. They do well at following the rules. I think lots of them work in hotels and banks."

"Yeah, especially hotels. They suffer from the 'you can't check in because it's not time yet and so I can't keep your bag because you haven't checked in, but you can't check in because it's not time yet' syndrome.

"Another group would be those who base what they learn about people only on what they see. So if they only see you when you are reading, they assume you are a studious person, but if they only see you when you are drinking wine, they assume you are a heavy drinker.

"Then there are those who take in all that they see, but feel that there is always something missing. They go looking for the missing piece. They are always sure there is one, and a missing piece means a surprise.

"No one has to prepare for a good surprise.

"Good surprises don't cause damage. But bad surprises can be devastating, so we protect ourselves by imagining what they might be.

"These information gatherers make it their business to speculate what possible negative the missing piece could be.

"Soon they determine the missing piece is not only negative. It becomes a truth, a bad truth that needs to be shared so that it can be defended against and squashed completely—even though it never existed. I've seen lots of kittens killed by people who have righteously marched off to slay a non-existent dragon."

Larry nodded knowingly. "Most people do that one at some time, particularly when they are feeling insecure. No one likes to be blindsided by a negative."

"Yeah, I can understand it. It's a form of self-preservation. What's a more basic instinct than that? I've done it too. I've learned two things. Whenever I act without knowing, I hurt someone. Whenever I feel righteous, I am wrong."

"Then a fourth group would be the folks who know the rules. They follow the more noticeable and accepted way of finding out about other people. They use small talk. What I've found out about small talk is that it has a lot in common with the recipe for making a peanut butter and jelly sandwich."

"What'd you mean 'a lot in common with a recipe for a peanut butter sandwich'?" Larry asked, sincerely missing the analogy.

"Tell me, how many ways are there to make a PBJ sandwich?"

"One. You put—" he started.

"Might as well stop right there," I interrupted. "Ask five people and you'll get five different ways to make a peanut butter and jelly sandwich. Even better, every person will think that their way is the only way to do it. Wanna try?"

For the fun of it, since we were in the kind of place that invited pretense and interaction, we recruited a few people just to test our theory. We told them we were on a secret mission: could they tell us how to make a peanut butter and jelly sandwich? Thinking it was some sort of code identification system, they each answered without thinking us crazy for asking, and every answer was different.

"See."

"Wow."

"My point was that people feel the same way about small talk. Everyone has their own definition of what it is, and what its purpose is. I bring it up in this discussion because the one point everyone seems to agree on is that it's one way that people get information about each other, and figure out where each other's boundaries lie.

"As you might guess, I don't do small talk very well. I'm usually one step behind, two steps too serious, three steps too curious, and six steps too clever and comical than the situation or statement requires, which is WAY worse than not talking at all. So small talk starts and I get busy doing something else. One-on-one I find it painful just knowing that at any minute I might pick up the wrong verbal fork and stab myself in the foot. How's that for a mixed metaphor?" I ended proudly.

"Yeah, you're not a small talker, but then I've never heard of anyone winning the Nobel Prize for small talk. So I think there might be bigger worries in life. People worth knowing seem to understand you fine," Larry smiled. "Even the dog has a soft spot for you. . . . Keep going, this is getting interesting."

"I think there are only two groups left—those who learn through intuition, and the observers. I'm the first. I think you're probably the second. Together the two are sort of a yin and yang of information.

"Those of us who use intuition seem to get information from the air. We can see things in people's eyes, but can't tell you how we see it. Somehow we know what they're thinking and feeling, but we're not sure how we know. It works really well when we're personally feeling secure. It's not so good when we're feeling insecure, because then we start second-guessing everything we think we see, and everything we really do see—a closed door, a person who doesn't say 'hello', a friend who forgets to call—gets assigned a deeper meaning whether it actually has one or not.

"Those who rely on observation can actually explain how you know what you know, but can get misled by the very data you're looking for. It's the exception that proves the rule that can undo your analysis of a person. The thief who really does believe in honor screws up the equation. The very contradictions in human nature make quantifying observation difficult."

"So people who think like me need people who think like you for balance, and vice versa," Larry put in with a smile.

"Is this where Barbra Streisand comes in to sing?"

"Nah, I don't need her to make my points for me."

"So your point is that my friends need my perspective as much as I need theirs."

"Ding, score one for the little dancer with the curious eyes and the sun that rises on her head."

"And I need my friends' perspective to have a balanced picture of the world."

"Ding, score another one for the super spy whose father hung the moon."

"And you are just some misguided nice guy, who for some reason thinks it's his job to make sure that I'm happy."

"Ding, ding, and ding! We have a winner here, ladies and gentleman! And what do we have tonight, Chet, for our mind-running little lady from Chicago who knows five ways to make a peanut butter and jelly sandwich and has come all this way to play and win our game?" Larry said energetically.

Then, deepening his voice, Larry continued talking as imaginary announcer Chet. "Well, Larry, we have the undying esteem of her newest lifelong friend and a ride back to Chicago with a handsome line-dancing cowboy, in a magnificent 1934 Packard V-12 Cabriolet Touring Car."

I liked the part where he called himself my newest lifelong friend.

A human being came to collect our money as Larry was giving his Chet speech. A real person. Hmmmm. I guessed the mechanical hand hadn't been vetted to handle the money. I had heard that mechanical hands had problems with maintaining their loyalties in the world of espionage. I would have bet that they were masters at what we used to call the five-finger discount. I guessed it made sense to keep them away from the money.

Larry handed over his credit card without breaking the storyline. So I stayed in the story right along with him.

"Darn," I said, hanging my head and trying to look my best imitation of TV-game-show disappointed. "I've already got one of those. Well, I suppose I could sell it to my sister after the show. Of course, she died before I was born. So I don't 'spose I'd get much."

"Oh Chet, it looks like we have an unhappy winner," Larry said in his Larry-game-show voice. "What can we do for this lady who's finally remembering what it's like to have fun?"

"Well, Larry," Larry said in his deep Chet voice. "We could let her choose door number 1, door number 2, door number 3 or the box before which Harold Barrel is standing."

"No thank you," I said, doing my best TV-game-show weeping.

"Hey, Chet," Larry said. "It's a no-go. I'm onto Plan C."

He then changed to Chet and said, "Good luck."

"All right, what do you want?" Larry asked.

I smiled my curious dancer, Alice-in-Wonderland, aspiring-angel-Angela, Richard's evil-twin smile, and said, "The truth, the whole truth and nothing but the truth. Starting with why you didn't bring the dog . . . "

Chapter Twenty two

My Story Is Your Story

WE LEFT THE RESTAURANT through the phone booth. It cost us each a quarter to take that way. It opened out to a walkway along the river. I needed a few minutes to get my bearings, but Larry apparently knew exactly where he was. He started heading off in the direction of his car.

I cleared my throat, and said, "Excuse me, mind if I join you?"

"Sorry," he said. "I'm used to traveling alone, invisible and ignored. Here, please take my arm. We'll walk slow and enjoy the night sky by the river."

"Don't think you can stall too long," I said, though I was quite content to enjoy the walk, the sky, the night before hearing his tale. After all, I had waited this long. What was a few minutes longer? Still, I felt the missing presence of the dog.

"Stop," Larry said.

"Stop what?"

"Stop thinking about the dog," he answered.

"What? I can't think about the dog either?"

"It's just not a good idea, right now," he said practically in a whisper.

"Did that safe house have a paranoid effect on your brain?" I stopped walking, and turned to face him. "There's no one around. You don't need to whisper. We're all alone. Look at that sky!"

I walked over to the side of the walkway to peer into the water. It was like being able to see the sky above and below me. Whatever was on Larry's mind, my mind was free and flying.

"Come over, come look at this, Larry," I called. He seemed to have let go of whatever he'd been whispering about, and returned to the Larry I'd come to enjoy sharing bits of life with.

"Imagine a planet that had sky both above and below it," I said wistfully. "Wouldn't that be cool?"

"You mean, something like . . . uh," he hesitated just the perfect second, then said, "Earth?"

"You know what I mean, where you could actually see sky all around you."

"There's always skydiving," he said.

"Yeah, right after I sleep in a coffin, ride in a submarine, and do every other thing that my body says 'not a good idea' to," I said, backing away from the water view and continuing to walk backward in the direction we had been going.

For some reason I really enjoy walking backwards at night. It reminds me of dancing, and in this case it let me see Larry's face while we were talking. Of course, it also meant I had to trust him to tell me if I was approaching the edge of the planet and was about to fall into the abyss, but I figured I was fairly safe on that count.

I was just about to turn my head to the sky and start spinning around with my arms out like a first grader, when Larry said, "Stop, it's time to cross the street."

"Mind if I turn a few times first?"

"Not at all, take your time."

"Never mind. It's not as much fun when it's not spontaneous."

Instead, I took his arm, and in a few minutes we were at the repair shop, unlocking the door, and I was getting settled in the Packard while Larry wrote a note of thanks to Jack. He probably thought I didn't see him leave a few bills of American currency, most likely designated for those little girls of Jack's Larry had mentioned earlier.

Before getting in the car, Larry reached in the back for his driving cap, which reminded me to put on my Audrey Hepburn babushka. Putting on his hat as he dropped into the driver's seat, he started up the car in one almost seamless motion, and we were off. The automatic garage door opened as if it had been awaiting his approach and departure—which I guess you could argue that it was—and the road rose up to meet us as if it were awaiting the feel of his tires—which I guess you could argue it was too.

Whether by accident or intent or serendipity, when Larry turned on the music to play us out of Milwaukee, it repeated "White Sun," the last song again, which was nicely circular and just fine with me.

> *And I slip away down by the water*
> *And I slip away down by the sea*
> *Take love and give love*
> *It's got to be.*[6]

I relax into the night. I think of how every person should have a place to slip away to and I slip away to mine under the sky. Somewhere on the back roads I come back to the car and realize that it's not my hair follicles that are getting noisy and self-conscious, but Larry's.

"Larry, who put a quarter in you tonight?" I asked. "You're all wound and weirding. That's supposed to be my job. What's going on? Does this have something to do with the dog?" I asked.

"Shh," he said. "I'll tell you, but you need to understand something. My friend, the one you keep mentioning and asking about. He doesn't know what I'm about to tell you. If when you hear the whole story, you want to tell him, that's fine, but it should be an informed decision."

"There you go talking in code again," I said, and I gave him what to me had become the requisite sock in the shoulder as a reminder.

"Hopefully, I'll be done with that soon. The problem I'm wrestling with is that I don't quite know how to start. What I'm about to tell you is a story of your own making, but my aspiring-angel-to-be, you're going to need more than a little faith and imagination, you're going to need the whole sky and all of your memories to understand it."

I socked his shoulder again. "You probably should begin."

"Well, you were running through your memories to find some balance, right? It's not surprising that balance would be a quest for you. If I ask you what your mother taught you," Larry asked, "what would you say?"

"She taught me everything I know about strength."

"And your father?"

"Everything I know about love."

"Well, that's where my story begins," Larry said, turning off the music. I sat back and closed my eyes to picture the story as he told it.

⊰⊱ ⊰⊱ ⊰⊱

Once upon a time there was this very strong boy. His father had died, and he felt himself to be the man of the house. This boy loved his mother deeply, but held no quarter with her boyfriend. So, being his own man, he left home and school after 6th grade to make a life for himself. He didn't go far—no more than 30 miles—and he checked in on his mother, his brother and his little sister, whenever the boyfriend wasn't around, because he was the oldest son and that's what oldest sons do.

His new life wasn't easy. He took very hard jobs for little money, because he was still a boy, an immigrant's child at that, and this was barely past the turn of the twentieth century. Yet, he made his way through his teenage years, and through the Great Depression, to become an adult. And on the day prohibition was repealed, he and a partner opened a business of their own—a saloon.

I guess you could say he had made it. He was what you might call a good-looking eligible bachelor. But he was also still a young guy. There were no great romances. His work was his social life. He could take care of his mother, and feel secure that there would always be food on the table.

This boy, now a man, was well into his late thirties when he fell in love with a beautiful young lady, thirteen years younger. He loved her because she was smart, and sensitive, and brave, and full of life. He loved her because she, like he, was her own person. He loved her because she had worked as hard as he had to be who she was. His only wish was that she was happy. They got married and soon had two beautiful sons.

⋇ ⋇ ⋇

"My brothers," I said.

"Yes, your brothers," he said.

⋇ ⋇ ⋇

They weren't exceptionally rich, but they were rich in spirit and rich with life. They owned their house. They owned their business. They owned themselves. The man had everything he wanted, except for one thing. A daughter, a beautiful daughter, a mirror of her mother.

They had a daughter, but something went wrong. She died nine days after she was born.

❦   ❦   ❦

"My sister. My mom told me about her when I was eight." I left the story for a while to think about what I already knew.

Most people, I suppose, don't understand what it is like to lose a baby that has gone full term. I don't. I've thought about it. It must be a very personal thing. I would guess that one mother can't even imagine another mother's sense of loss. How would you find your way back from that loss? How would you recognize joy when it came again? How would you explain the sadness you felt to your two young sons? Who could predict or explain the impact such an event must have had on the relationships around you? What little nuances, what big feelings might have occurred or changed had that event turned out differently?

Larry drove on in the darkness with only the glow of the dash lights offering comfort. He seemed to know when I was ready to listen again.

❦   ❦   ❦

It was a very sad time for a while. The world that had been so full of life seemed to be one at loose ends. The man tried to make the sun rise and set on her head, but she only saw the rain. The little boys had each other and their dad and school and a big backyard to keep them alive, but the beautiful young lady had lost some of the life in her eyes. And the man had lost his chance for a beautiful daughter that was a mirror of the beautiful young lady that he loved.

The doctors had said that the beautiful young lady should not have any more babies. I don't know how she felt about that, but she never said yes to the operation.

Then, as sometimes happens in the ways of heaven and the world, a miracle occurred. Three years later, almost to the day, the beautiful young lady gave birth to another baby girl.

❧ ❧ ❧

"That would be me."

"Yes, that was you."

Larry stopped talking. He knew I would want to think on this too. I did.

A psychologist friend told me that they call a child that follows a baby that dies a replacement child. She said it's not unusual for a replacement to never quite feel that he or she has a right to be on this planet.

I thought of the remarkably close relationship I perceived between my older brothers, closer than that of any twins I knew. I wondered whether that was only the product of having shared a bedroom through high school, or perhaps something more. I thought of my relationship with my dad. Somehow we had a heartfelt bond forged in platinum never to hurt each other's feelings, yet I had no idea how we had gotten there—it just always has been.

❧ ❧ ❧

The man was so joyous he rented a 40-acre farm and hired an accordion band to play for a party to celebrate their new baby girl. And from that minute forward a bond was forged between daughter and dad that could never be broken. Even after he died.

Everywhere he went, if he could he took her with him. Everyone in town knew who she was and called her by name. The banker, the grocer, the lawyer, all treated her as his personal assistant with the respect of the heir apparent. And she learned the role of royalty to speak to all as her equal with respect and kindness, and to feel their pain.

But she was always aware that her dad was much older than other kids' dads. And being a very smart little girl she was always aware that one day he would die and leave her. One day she asked him about it.

≈ ≈ ≈

"Larry, I love this story, I really do, but you promised to tell me your story, not mine," I said. "And I need to go soon. Tonight is the night for the story. It's time. I want to know."

"I keep trying to explain, your story is my story," was all that he said. I was beginning to think it was a mantra for him.

"Okay, go on." I listened.

≈ ≈ ≈

The little girl used to go wherever he was to be with her dad when he would come home in the afternoons to rest. She would sit and talk with him about life and about dancing. Sometimes they would sing together. Sometimes he would tell her stories.

One day she said to him, "Daddy, how old are you?" He told her he was fifty-two. She said, "I'm only seven. That means when I go to college, you'll be sixty-two and when I graduate, you'll be sixty-six."

"That's right, and right again," he told her.

She thought on that for a long time, but she didn't talk about it. She didn't talk about it for a very long time. But she thought about it. She thought about how both of her grandfathers were dead before she was born. She thought about her sister who was in heaven before she was born. She thought about a world in which her dad wasn't there. She didn't want to think about it. She most certainly didn't want to talk about it. She pretended not to know about it. She was pretty good at pretending—after all, she was seven.

⇥⊱⊱⊱⊱⇥

By the time I had finished thinking about that, we were transported from the Packard into my condo and were sitting quietly on the floor in the living room with wine and an exclusive meal of the house—fresh French bread, baked brie, grapes and wine. The mostly silence made for a nice conversational transition. When we were settled and picking at our food, I started.

"Larry, you know that I think the world of you and the dog, right?" I said, looking him in his eyes, as I lit a candle.

"Yeah, I kind of got the feeling that you had gotten over your irritation with our interrupting your thoughts of nothing," he teased.

"Still, I know hardly anything about you. Well, let me put that right. I know a lot about you. I know you care about me enough to share your wisdom, to be a friend to my friends, to hang out and have fun. I know you have a good mind, a kind heart, and a dog friend who thinks the world of you and who knows how to keep you in line." I stopped.

Larry said, "Go on, curious Alice Angela. You deserve answers."

"It's just that I know all of these things, because I pay attention, not because you have shared them with me. Sorry, correction again. Technically you've shared them by doing them, but you've told me hardly anything about you or the dog. I don't even know your last name. I'm pretty sure it's not 'and the dog.' It's not, is it? Your full name is NOT Larry Andthedog?"

Larry laughed, "It could be, knowing you, but no, it's not."

"That's what I'm trying to say. I want—need—to know *your* story," I said. I gave no playful sock to the shoulder.

"I keep telling you. You made it up. My story is your story."

"You keep talking in code, as if I'm supposed to know what you're talking about. Help me out here. I'm clueless."

Then he just started rattling like an old Schwinn bicycle. "I suppose I could be hurt that you don't remember me, but you were awfully young. And then there was your dad. No one could catch your attention when your dad was around—or his either, for that matter," he said. "Of course, you've pretty much ignored me since, but then most of the world could say that." He finished his speech with a grand smile in his eyes to be sure I wouldn't be hurt by his words.

"So we were friends when I was little?" I asked, still trying to unravel this puzzle he was holding just out of my reach.

Larry got serious. "I guess I was somebody you could talk to when your dad wasn't around. Kind of like the song says, 'someone to watch over you'. Actually, it's good that we made it here before I finished my story, because the most important part of it is in that cedar chest right there."

The cedar chest Larry pointed to was sitting under my printer next to my desk.

"Ah," I said, "the elusive drawing you mentioned a while back. Name first, Mister. Then story. Then drawing. I'll keep quiet and eat my bread and cheese."

"My full name is Larry G. A. Mountain Star."

"What? Mountain Star? That's the meaning of my Dad's last name."

"I told you. You picked it. I came by that honestly."

"Wait," I said. "What does the G. A. stand for?" I asked.

"It does not stand for your father's first name. Okay? Could I tell you the rest of the story first, please?"

"Maybe you'd better."

❧ ❧ ❧

Eventually, after weeks of thinking about it, the little girl went back to her dad and asked him, "Daddy, when you die who will I talk to? Who will hug me when I'm sad? Who will make the sun rise? Who will hold the moon in the sky?"

The man, who only wanted her to be happy, took her

questions very seriously. He said, "We have a problem, don't we? Everyone has to die, and I'll have to wait for you in heaven. But what will we do in the meantime? Let's think on this problem. Hmmm. What do you usually do when you have a big problem like this?"

The little girl looked in her dad's eyes with so much love and said, "Sometimes I dance, sometimes I draw, sometimes I think and think until my head hurts."

"Well, that doesn't sound good," said her dad. "Sometimes I take a problem apart. Let's see, I'll be in heaven with God and the angels, so I'll have plenty of company until you get there. That seems okay, don't you think?"

"Uh-huh."

"But I can see where you'll have a problem, because you'll have to take care of your mom and your brothers, so you might need someone to talk to," he said sagely.

"Yeah," the little girl said, all seriousness. "Somebody like you."

"You could use a guardian angel, I think," her dad said.

Surprisingly she said, "Mom told me I have one. But I don't think I believe it."

"Oh I see," her Dad said. "What seems to be the problem with your guardian angel?"

"I make room for him when I go to sleep. I never see him. I talk to him. He never talks back," she explained. "I think he's made up, like Santa Claus."

"You could have gotten a dud angel," her dad said, "or maybe he's just shy, like you used to be. Maybe he needs to know you believe in him. What's his name? Ezekiel?"

"No," she said with a frown.

"Gabriel?"

"No," she said, with an even bigger frown.

"Does he have a name?"

"Well, yes, but I've never told anyone."

"Are you going to tell your dad? Or am I going to have to tickle it out of you?" her father said, quickly grabbing her as he was wont to do.

She giggled and said, "Larry, his name is Larry."

"Larry?" Her father's smile made his whole face light up. "And does this Larry have a proper full name?"

"Of course, he does, Daddy," she said, as if her father had lost his senses. "His name is Larry Guardian Angel Mountain Star. I named him after you."

"Tell me more," her father had said.

And so the little girl did. She told him that Larry was very tall, and very rich, and that he had three very special cars. She said he lived in Chicago somewhere, and that he could dance romantic dances and fun dances too. She said he knew how to laugh and how to listen and how to sing, and that he liked the sky. She told her father that he was good at organizing 64 *crayons, and that he knew exactly what to do when someone was sad.*

And then her father asked her to draw a picture of Larry so that he could see what Larry looked like. And she did.

❧ ❧ ❧

"Look in the cedar chest," Larry said. "It's at the very bottom."

And there it was . . . a picture—drawn by my-seven-year, old hand—of me holding hands with a very tall guy who looked very much like Larry and a dog who looked very much like the dog.

And the caption read
     Me   Larry   and the dog Daddy sent

Chapter Twenty three

The 65th Crayon

I PULLED MY HEADPHONES OFF and went to the cedar chest to see whether my drawing was really there. It was.

I pulled it out and sat on the floor next to the cedar chest for a very long time, holding that picture, just looking at that picture. I remembered it. I remembered drawing it with my box of 64 crayons. I remembered showing it to my dad. I remembered telling my dad about it. I told my dad that Larry was a lot like him, that Larry lived somewhere in Chicago, and that he had three wonderful movie-star cars so that we could go places. But most especially I remembered the dog.

My dad and I had talked about the picture after I drew it. I told him that I was worried that Larry might be lonely when I was busy at school or at dancing class. So he said that he would make sure that Larry had a dog to keep him company. I asked my dad to make sure it was a big dog, a wise dog, a dog with eyes the color of caramels and a heart as big as the world. From what I had seen this week, my dad had made a pretty good choice.

I went back to my chair and put my headphones back on. I needed to know more.

I'm not sure what Larry had been doing while I was catching up with the story of the picture, but he seemed ready enough to talk when I looked up. I noticed that most of the bread, cheese, and grapes were gone. He had moved to the rocking chair.

"Larry, I still don't understand why the dog couldn't be here," I said, choosing to sit on the floor.

"How can I say this? The dog doesn't know he isn't a dog. Well, that's not quite right. He's a dog all right. What he doesn't know is that he's not like other dogs," Larry tried his best to explain. The more he tried, the more the rocking chair he was sitting in moved back and forth.

"Are you saying he's a guardian-angel dog?"

"No, not that. There's no such thing. Actually, he's a memory of a dog, a particular dog that you had a relationship with. You and your dad used to visit the Flanagans' farm outside the tiny town where your dad grew up. The dog was the Flanagans' dog. Remember how you used to spend hours with the dog? He was the only dog you ever made friends with as a child. Haven't you noticed he shows up whenever you think of him? He never eats. He never sleeps. He responds to you and me exactly as you would want him to."

"You mean all of my life I've had access to the perfect dog pet, who understood me and loved me and never needed walking or cleaning up after, and no one ever told me?"

"That's true. If you want to see it that way," Larry said.

"I miss him. Can I think him back?" I asked.

"Sure, go for it," Larry said.

Before Larry was done talking the dog was with us.

It felt like a family reunion to have him back with us again. I put on a new playlist I thought appropriate, and I sat back on the floor, just to be close to the dog again. I couldn't quit touching him, and scratching him, and looking deep into those caramel eyes. It felt like sitting under the big oak tree in my backyard with my dad again.

I also wanted to know more about how this guardian-angel thing was supposed to work. Obviously I had been pretty bad at my part of the deal, if I hadn't even remembered that I had one—me of "the God is in His heaven, and angels are everywhere" fame. What was it that Larry had said about being used to being ignored?

"Larry, what did you mean when you said, 'I'm used to traveling alone, invisible and ignored'?" The dog heard that and moved next to Larry, placing his big lowercase 'd' head on Larry's foot, as if he were showing Larry that he knew Larry was there.

"Ah, that was nothing really. It's a hazard of the job, all GAs complain about it," he tried to brush it off. At the same time, he reached down to scratch the dog's head.

"But it doesn't make the job sound very fulfilling. Being a guardian angel should be fulfilling, one would think," I said, pulling my legs under me where I sat.

"Well, a lot of the time, it's pretty boring, to tell the truth. I mean, I'm *your* guardian angel, for God's sake. You don't seem to need anything most of the time. So what am I good for—a crayon sorter? You don't even color much anymore. The dog and I spend a lot of time watching people, and thinking about when you were little."

My guardian angel was complaining about his working conditions. This was too weird. The dog watched my face to see whether I was okay. I was busy watching Larry's face for the same reason.

"Tell me I'm unpredictable, too polite, too tall, and too cranky, and you're history, mister," I said, half-sitting, half-leaning on one arm, trying to tease him out of his funk. "How is this guardian-angel-person thing supposed to work?"

"Well, I don't know for sure, because I've only been *your* guardian angel. Don't get me wrong. I knew going in that no one could follow an act like your dad's. Still, now that I've finally had a chance to try my wings—no pun intended—I've been thinking that what we had going this week was pretty productive. We got you having fun without thinking, despite yourself."

"Right on all counts. You're a darn good guardian angel, even if I did make you up myself," I smiled, sitting up again.

"Yeah, well, before you burst into joyous flames, remember that you also forgot about me and left me to rot—so don't be feeling too pleased with yourself, Ms. Alice," Larry countered.

"I don't often feel pleased with myself. I've spent most of my life feeling like the 65th crayon in a box of 64—that one that's the wrong size to fit the sharpener; the one that when you do get it to go in, it never quite gets the point, like the others do. In fact, it usually breaks off in the sharpener and ruins the sharpener for all of the rest," I said, leaning back against the cedar chest, putting my legs straight out in front of me, and my chin to my chest. The dog moved next to me, and laid himself out long and lean with his head on his paws.

"I've already said that I think people are loony. But that aside, you might take heart in knowing that almost everyone feels that way a good part of the time," he offered. "Feeling like you don't fit is part of life. Making mistakes and breaking things are too.

"If it helps, Miss Crayon 65," Larry continued. "You're not the only one. Most of us feel like the 65th Crayon at some time or another. When you feel that way, try to remember the Sacred Realities of the 65th Crayon," he said, handing me a card on which they were written.

The Sacred Realities of the 65th Crayon

1. *The 65th crayon is self-sharpening. It is, and always will be, sharp enough already.*

2. *The 65th crayon was not created to make a point, to get a point, or to point out anything.*

3. *The 65th crayon blends and balances other colors, coaxing out their most vibrant shades.*

4. *The 65th crayon would not fit, even in the empty box.*
    The 65th crayon is the perfect size to fit in the whole world.

5. *The 65th crayon is the most unique and thus the most*
    precious crayon of the set.

6. *The 65th crayon may get misplaced or given away,*
    but it is never lost.

"But what do the sacred realities mean?"

"They mean you're already everything you need to be."

I looked at the card for a long time, making sense of each point on its own. I had to admit I did feel better. I was getting a sense that I did belong.

"But why this time? Why did you show up now? After all of these years?" I asked, again pulling my legs close to my chest.

"This was the first time that you left enough space for me to help. In fact, I was so surprised, I almost didn't know what to do," he admitted. A "yip" from the dog confirmed Larry's read on the situation.

Apparently I just hadn't made room for them in my life before this. It made sense. I had hardly squeezed out room for myself.

"So now what do we do?" I wondered aloud, wishing for any answer that kept us together.

"Well, you need to understand that I'm not the answer. I'm only a guide, here to help you find the answers. You still have to find balance in your life. I can only help you get there."

"I know, you're not my dad, and you can't live my life for me. Got it," I summarized, then a spark in me ignited. "And nobody's gonna die and we're still gonna dance tomorrow."

"What?" Larry asked, but I swear the dog knew exactly where I was coming from.

"Oh nothing, that's just a saying I picked up from someone I used to be. It's a good philosophy, don't you think? . . . In any case, I have to go to work tomorrow, and I'm starting to get nervous that . . . that I . . . uh . . . that I still haven't picked out what I'm going to wear," I said, deflecting from what was really on my mind.

"But first, would it be okay if I cut to the chase this one time, and just ask what I need to know?" I asked Larry with as much grace as I could pull together after a day of revelations.

"Hey, direct is eons more delightful than being ignored. Please do," Larry said. The dog, showing his support for my cause, sidled up right next to me.

"What are our options moving forward?" I asked.

"What?" Larry looked totally perplexed.

"I don't mean to sound like I'm negotiating a contract, but you said I could be direct. I don't know how else to say what I mean. Where do we go from here? Are there choices? If so, what are they? I know I still have work to do. And I also have everything at work to deal with. I'm not sure what I'm going to do about my boss and the bad things that are happening. I'm wondering . . . Will you and the dog be here to help me? There. I said it," I answered with all sincerity, pulling my legs even closer to my chest and resting my chin on my knees. A big lowercase 'd' head popped up next to my own.

"Well, I can see some options, as you put it. The first is that I convince you that the dog and I were just something you imagined on one of your runs, which we kind of are," he smiled. "Then we go back to watching you from afar, ready to catch you if things get dangerous."

"Not likely I'm choosing that one," I replied.

He said, "Yeah, that's what I figured."

"The second is that I convince you that my name is really Mike and the dog's name is Shiner. We meet you in real life and I slowly use angel tricks to get you to forget all of this guardian angel stuff we've shared," Larry offered. "We develop a human friendship that runs a regular human friendship life cycle."

"Absolutely not! I could never give up my guardian angel. Even if I did forget you once," I said, slamming my legs flat and my hands to my sides, but still wishing for an answer that kept our little family together.

"Then I guess we're left with option three. We could agree to work together as angel, person, and dog to get your life in order," he said, with that Dennis Quaid glint in his eye once again. The dog rolled over on his back and offered his tummy. "You would have to keep my actual GA status confidential. You probably shouldn't tell your friends about me."

I said, "Now that one works for me. Larry, I can keep that secret as long as you're nearby."

"Then I'll take the dog and the Packard home to 'somewhere in Chicago'. You could have been a bit more specific, you know. Every night I have to invent a neighborhood called *Somewhere*," Larry said.

"At least I didn't make it somewhere over the rainbow," I laughed.

I pulled off my headphones and as I set them on the desk I saw something under my keyboard. I pulled it out. It was a card of the Sacred Realities of the 65th Crayon.

Chapter Twenty four

Gunning for Bear

IT WAS WEDNESDAY. No need for details. By now you know the drill. I picked my clothes for work and hit the sheets. I fell asleep reading the list of Sacred Realities of the 65th Crayon. I awoke in the morning heartened, and knowing them by heart. I did a different morning transition routine.

Rather than run, I sat over coffee thinking about how I might apply the Crayon realities to my work life. Twenty minutes into my workday, I realized it was going to take more than thinking about how to change things at work if I wanted to make them better.

I'm not quite sure how people do it, but I've noticed that it is quite possible to go gunning for bear and never actually carry a weapon—only words. If you're the bear they're gunning for, I suppose that doesn't really matter . . . a weapon is a weapon is a weapon.

I was sitting at my computer, working on some editorial changes for a project that was on a fairly short timeline, when my boss stopped by under the guise of a kind and caring person.

"Are you okay?" he asked. He looked deeply-concerned and, for the life of me, I couldn't figure out why he would be concerned to start with.

"Yes," I said. "I've been following your advice and looking for balance in my life. I had dinner with a friend last night, and a great conversation. It was nice."

"I'm so glad you're finding people outside of work to share your problems with," he said—but I was distracted by his eyes, they were saying something else. "Because your team is young. You don't want to burden them with things that might concern you here at work. They don't need to worry about what you worry about. They're not paid to do so."

Concerns? Worries? What concerns? Worries? What worries? What was he talking about? He had no idea about anything that might be bothering me.

I looked in his eyes again. I had been wrong. His eyes were not saying something different. His eyes were saying nothing at all. They were just watching me to see how I would react.

"I'm not sure I know what you're talking about," I said, making sure that my eyes didn't show anything I was thinking.

"Well, for example, I noticed you had lunch yesterday with

Mitch. He's a young, impressionable guy," my very big boss said, his eyes showing no concern for Mitch or me.

"Yes, I did. We talked about his newly born niece and what it's like to watch kids grow up. He had the salad. I had the tuna salad sandwich. I paid. He left the tip. We were gone about 40 minutes," I replied matter-of-factly, with not a care on my face.

"You shouldn't tell him not to talk to me," this "superior" of mine said. It was ludicrous.

"I didn't tell him not to talk to you. I wouldn't tell him not to talk to you. I trust him. I trust you. Why would I tell him not to talk to you?" I said as clearly and as evenly as I might.

"Well, that's good. That's how it should be," said my boss, with false cheerfulness and that same smile that didn't reach his eyes.

I have often wondered at how many people seem to use this half smile and why it seems to work for them. I not only find it distracting, I find it scary, in the way of witches in fairy tales. Why don't other people seem to react to these partial smiles? Does a smile that doesn't make it to your eyes really fool people? Could such a smile actually be sincere? Or could everyone be pretending to believe in each other's facial expressions?

Maybe the people who don't smile with their eyes don't even know that they are not fully sincere. It was possible. After all, you do something long enough, it feels right and natural. These "smile-for-a-purpose smiles" are a most curious thing to me, whatever the case. I get extremely uncomfortable whenever I see that contradictory smile, despite my otherwise high regard and good feelings for a person, despite whether I even know the person at all.

Then he said, "How's that special-projects budget coming along?"

"Special-projects budget?" I asked, knowing without knowing exactly what was about to follow. This kind of bomb-dropping was not new to me.

"Did I forget to tell you? I'm sorry. Actually I just found out myself last Monday. We need a full roll-out of all special projects for the next five years, including cost breakouts and return-on-investment projections by Thursday's Executive Committee Meeting. So I'll need your part by Tuesday latest." He actually said this with a smile. I couldn't tell whether he was clueless or enjoying himself. But the smile didn't make it up to his eyes.

"In order to do that, it might help to meet first to make decisions on which projects we actually think we'll invest in. It would save us both some time in the long run," I suggested.

"Don't worry about me," he said through the same smile. "I don't mind reading a few extra lines of spreadsheet to consider the options. Besides, I'm triple-booked all week. Can't meet until Tuesday anyway."

I had just been handed about 30-40 hours of extra work due in less than a week. Why was it that I had thought I loved this job?

"What if I shoot you a short list of the projects that I propose that we pursue, and their timelines?" I said with a proactive, professional air.

"Nah, don't bother," he said, smile still stuck. "Just go with the list you have. We'll review and chop the budget on Tuesday. Thanks. You're a big help. Gotta go."

My first thought was *what just happened?* My second was *no wonder my people think I'm cranky and unpredictable. Who wouldn't be?* My third was to look at the clock. It was only 9:00 a.m., and I was already miserable.

And worse, there weren't any signs that work was getting better. At least when the Shamrock Princess in the photo woke up the next morning, the itchy dress and the people taking pictures were gone. Hearing my thoughts, I started to picture myself wearing "needy pink." This was not good. This was not good at all.

Larry's words came back to me. "Or maybe you were braver," he had said.

What had happened to me? I didn't feel brave. I didn't feel curious. I didn't feel balanced. I didn't even feel angry.

I felt tired.

I started to fantasize over some sort of nondescript illness.

> *HEADLINE NEWS: Woman With Too Many Projects Checks into Celebrity Rehab for Exhaustion. Tune in Tonight at 11.*

I knew all too well that an over-achiever's idea of a vacation always included a hospital. At least in this fantasy I had upgraded to the movie star version where I could wear nice clothes, sit on a beach, drink cold beverages, and have a pair of good looking young resort workers . . . er . . . caretakers . . . fan me and feed me grapes.

That got me through to 9:10.

Only seven hours to go.

Then I remembered the Sacred Realities of the 65th Crayon. I was self-sharpening and sharp enough already. I didn't need to make a point, to get a point, or to point out anything. I could blend and balance spreadsheets and stuff. I fit just perfectly in the world, even when the box I worked in felt a little cramped. I am unique and I am never lost.

That was better.

I thought about spreadsheets. I actually liked spreadsheets. When I could climb into one, it was a little like running in my mind. Put on my headphones and crawl into the numbers. I could do this. I just had to keep my focus and hold onto to my head. I got started. Six hours later that budget had form and even a little style. It was just past time to go home.

"Hey you," my friend Craig looked in to say. "I haven't seen you around all day. I wasn't sure you were in."

"Been working on the SP budget all day. Benny said it's got to be done by Thursday, so he wants it by Tuesday," I said, finally taking a minute to breathe, just realizing I hadn't stopped for lunch or a bathroom break.

"Check in with him again on that," Craig said. "That Thursday Executive Committee meeting got put off yesterday. It's not happening until next month."

"Thanks for the news," I said cheerfully to Craig. He was a good guy, always making sure everyone was up-to-date with the latest communications.

As soon as he left, however, I said, "Grrrrr." A whole ticker tape of comments flew through my mind until all I could see was the color red and the words *dirty, pig-dog bastard.*

I stared out the window at my little blue car in rock-star parking, feeling like the farthest thing from a rock star until it was dark.

I printed out the draft of the budget I had finished. I put it in a file folder, wrote a message and stuck it on the outside.

Then I grabbed my stuff to head home, thinking of Larry already so that he might actually meet me there. On my way out, I slid the file folder under my boss's door. The sticky note on it said:

> *Benny,*
> *Craig told me that the Executive Committee Mtg. is postponed.*
> *Here's a draft of the Special Projects Budget.*
> *Something came up. I need to take two personal days—*
> *tomorrow and Friday. If you need me, call my cell.*
>
> *—A.*

I was beginning to see how people could go gunning for bear without a gun. And how I might disarm them.

Chapter Twenty five

Everyone's Eyes

WHEN I GOT HOME AND PUT ON my headphones, Larry and the dog were waiting for me with two pizzas just the way I like them.

"Thank you, thank you, thank you," I said, "for hearing what I wasn't saying."

To which Larry replied, "Hey, one 'Grrrr' from you travels at light speed, and one from your stomach runs it a close second." The dog jumped in mid-air, as if encouraging me.

I felt like I had my own personal cheering section. I guess you could argue that I did. Too bad I hadn't remembered these guys earlier . . . earlier in the day, and earlier in my life—and again my friend Nancy's words rang in my ears, "Sometimes you are so fast, and sometimes you are soooo slooooow."

We three decided to picnic on pizza in the living room. So I laid out an old plaid blanket with picnic paraphernalia and added the mandatory bottle of wine. I put a playlist on the surround-sound and pillows on the floor.

I gave Larry a three-minute summary of my day at work, or rather my day of busy-work, and thanked him for the gift of the Sacred Realities of the 65th Crayon one more time.

"I watched Benny's eyes, Larry. They were both dead and denying what he was saying. It was distracting. It was like trying to keep track of two unrelated conversations at the same time. His words were all cashmere and fireplaces, and his face was all threadbare and ashes. I was totally disarmed. I knew what was happening and I sat unable to respond to what I saw, because I had to respond to what he said."

"Eat your pizza," Larry said.

"I can't," I said, now staring at the wall. I wasn't pouting, but I wanted to be.

"Why not?" he asked, while choosing his next piece.

"I'm too busy thinking." The dog moved by me so that I would look at him and quit thinking.

"Well, stop thinking. Listen to the music and eat your pizza. Then go back to thinking again when you have some fuel," Larry advised.

And wouldn't you know it, the Mindy Smith song "Down in Flames" came on—how did that always happen? Did I subconsciously pre-program the music I needed to hear?—however it happened, when I heard the lyrics telling me about losing the chance to talk to angel, what could I do, but listen to the music?

. . . and eat my pizza?

. . . and pet the dog?

I listened to the next two or three songs and ate the next two or three pieces of pizza, and kept petting the dog. Larry was right. I did need the fuel. I felt better. I think Larry and the dog felt better too.

"Thanks, Larry," I said. Then I took the dog's face in my hands, put my face in his, and said, "Thanks to you, too, dog."

I tried to figure out exactly what it was that was bothering me. And I realized that it was that I didn't know how I felt about what happened today. Had I gotten so good at changing my paradigm that I didn't know what I really felt anymore? Had I so lost track of myself that my only response was "let me check in on my feelings and I'll get back to you later?"

"So, Crayon, what's the problem?" Larry started.

"Maybe I've gotten so good at blending the other colors that I don't know what color I am anymore. I don't like that I just sat there and took it, but I don't know what I should have done. I look at the real people around me—the ones who don't have to think about things to know how they feel—but I can tell you, how today's scenario would have been different for them."

"Tell me," Larry said.

"Benny just wouldn't have tried that game on Craig. He wouldn't have tried that with anyone he respects. It wouldn't have crossed his mind to act that way with the worker bees. They need to see him as the benevolent ruler—the giver of all that is good. If he made the mistake of trying it with Marlene, she would have said something like 'Are you crazy?' Then when she found out that he knew the meeting was canceled, she would have given it to him with both barrels. In fact, I just can't think of anyone who would have gotten the same scenario. Something I do or don't do makes me a target."

"Well, I suppose if you just sit there and don't respond, you might actually look like a target, especially to someone who feels like shooting at you," Larry observed.

"That's a problem. I don't want to be a target. Not anymore, not ever again," I declared.

"You know, not to sound silly, but people are only human. Maybe it makes them nervous that you don't respond. Maybe they start pushing to get a response, and keep pushing harder and harder, because they don't get one."

"What you're saying makes sense, you know," I admitted. "People wouldn't have to start out mad. By the time they've pushed for a while and still gotten no response, they're bound to think I'm just being resistant, or arrogant, or something, and end up being mad over that. Then it's self-justifying . . . I deserve to be a target for being so whatever."

"Yep, without knowing it, you could be asking them to shoot at you," Larry agreed.

"One part of the problem is I don't know where to draw the line. People do rude or hurtful things, and I don't tell them. First, I'm just being generous. Then I'm letting it go. Then I'm giving it the benefit of the doubt. Next thing you know, if I say something, it would make me look small, so I rise above it. Until, if I got mad, there's no way that it wouldn't be called an overreaction. So I'm left with no appropriate response.

"When it's a surprise attack like today, I'm truly lost," I continued. "I can't find a response. I get lost between the words and the eyeful intent. I end up so far inside myself, trying to figure it out, that I can't find my way back to the surface in time to answer. The best I can do is to say 'stop' with my eyes."

"Then we better get to work rewiring your heart to your brain," Larry said softly. "Crayon, you said you forgot what color you are. You're not just one color. You're every color and every nuance of color. Just because your response looks like no response, doesn't mean you don't have one. . . . Unfortunately, most folks can't see a line you draw in invisible ink. You have to leave the Safe House and deliver your messages so that the world can read them loud and clear." Larry had this metaphor thing down. There was no question about that.

Now how am I going to do that?

"How can I deliver my messages loud and clear when I can't even draw a line?"

"That is a problem," Larry said, beginning to sound a bit like my dad. The dog tilted his head in recognition. I think he thought so too.

"So are you going to dance, or draw, or think until your head hurts?" Larry asked, sweetly and sincerely reminding me of how I had told my dad I worked on problems once so long ago.

"I'm too self-conscious to dance, and I don't have any crayons," I said.

"That's sad. Maybe we should just take the problem apart. You know, you actually did respond today. You left a budget and note. Maybe you're just not comfortable with the response you made," Larry suggested.

"I'll buy that. I feel like my response was too much too late. Somehow I still see Benny with all of the power, like I'm the one who did something wrong," I said.

"So what it is that you did wrong?" Larry said.

"Nothing. Not a darn thing," I said, looking the dog right in the eyes. "I delivered more than was asked and took two personal days for the first time in more years than I care to count. Still I feel anxious and guilty, like something awful is going to happen."

"So *you* think you're a target too," he said.

"What?"

"You're planning on getting shot at," he gently pointed out.

He was right. I was. Not only was I planning on it. I was already feeling helpless about avoiding it.

"Oh God, I feel like such a fool. . . . I'm listening. But how do we rewire my heart to my head without killing me with all of my feelings colliding with all of the feelings I see in everyone's eyes?"

"You could learn, I bet," Larry said. "You're brave."

"I'm not so sure. Do you know, I was over 30 before I figured out that people had boundaries? People had been giving me the whole story in their eyes. I looked right past their boundaries. Of course, from their point of view, I was walking on every rule of how trust gets established. How embarrassing. How rude. No wonder people didn't know what to do with me," I murmured. "And, I never made any boundaries of my own."

"I can't make eye contact without seeing what people are thinking or feeling, and I can't hold a conversation without that information distracting me. Some of what I see are things that people don't want me to know—or worse, things that they haven't told themselves. So I steer clear of feelings and private thoughts. They're dangerous territory for me."

That was enough talk about that. I could feel my blood in my veins. It felt as if my body was somehow holding itself together after my skin had been pulled off. Worse than naked, more exposed than exposed, I longed to disappear. Perhaps a cloister was the answer. I started thinking of the Alan Parsons song, "Silence and I." I had to admit that Larry, the dog, and I seemed to be three of a kind, and we all had a kinship with silence.

Larry and the dog waited a respectful moment or so. They seemed to know I was somewhere inside myself again.

"Feelings are dangerous territory for everyone," Larry put in. "Every part of life is dangerous. You know you can't just crawl inside your head, hoping that folks who love you will stop by your skull for a visit every now and then. "

"Yeah, I know. Most days, my skull is too crowded for me. . . . and it creaks when you and the dog show up," I said, feeling relief at the image of people knocking at my skull. "But inside my head, I don't have to watch to be sure I don't trip over someone's feelings. I don't have to track what everyone sees versus what only I can see. . . . "

Larry made an off-hand remark, "It's a wonder how your lifelong friends put up with you. You're such a hateful creature."

"I don't know how to look in someone's eyes and not see what they don't want me to see," I confessed.

"Yep, hateful, definitely unredeemable and hateful," Larry said, shaking his head. "Don't you agree, dog?" The dog gave his single yip of agreement.

"I can't care as much as I want to care, because I'm not supposed to see what I see. Yet, I can't stop looking because then things I do make people think that I don't care at all," I moaned. "The only option left is to buy out completely. Refuse to compete. Decide not to participate."

"Seriously. What you're saying is that you have decided to stop seeing the world, because it causes you problems," Larry said. "That's just not an option. That leaves a hole in the world, and a hole in you."

We were all silent. I knew I couldn't explain my way out of what I had said. I cared. I cared deeply. I couldn't fit in. So, like they did in grade school pull-out programs, I had pulled myself out of the world. I was downstairs safely sorting library books while the rest of the world was having a life.

"So, Dr. Larry and Dr. 'd' dog, do you have another solution for me, or am I stuck in my head forever?"

Larry looked at the dog. The dog looked at Larry. They put their faces nose-to-nose, as if in conference. They turned their heads in tandem and looked at me. Then they looked at each other. I'd swear I saw them wink. Then they turned to consider the lake for a very long time. I think it was five or six songs worth of a long time. I watched the lake for that long time too.

I was replaying the whole conversation in my head. The conversation came crashing down on me and I realized that I had started recording myself once again. I was making myself a poster child for self-incrimination, self-flagellation, and possible self-delusion. I felt lonely.

They were still looking at the lake.

Then . . . once again Larry looked at the dog. The dog looked at Larry. They put their faces nose-to-nose, as if in conference. Again they turned their heads in tandem and looked at me. Again they looked at each other, and again I'd swear I saw them wink. Then they looked at me for a very long time.

Finally one of them spoke.

"What's the name of the song playing now?" Larry asked.

"Huh?"

"This song, what's it called?" Larry asked again.

"It's called 'See the Innocence.' It's by Tommy Henriksen."

"Your world-renowned team of doctors, the dog and myself, have consulted, and that's our prescription."

"What do you mean, that's your prescription?"

"Don't stop seeing. See the innocence," Larry proclaimed, as if he played a doctor on TV. "Everyone loses too much when you choose not to participate. Instead, see the innocence in every pair of eyes. See the innocence in your own eyes. See the innocence, and there will be no boundaries to what people will see in you."

Until that moment, I had looked in everyone's eyes but my own.

Chapter Twenty six

Seeing the Innocence

SO I TOOK A LONG LOOK in the mirror.

I saw the innocence there.
I also saw that not everything in the world was about me.

No boundaries . . . funny how banana-hand Larry and that
make-it-clear dog had turned me around again. Suddenly, my
"no boundaries" sounded right.

Larry and the dog left me with my thoughts shortly after they
had made their prescription, telling me that if I still showed
symptoms of anxiety I should call them in the morning. I was
filled with hope. Their suggestion was so elegantly simple.
The answer was not to stop seeing. The answer was in what I
chose to see.

"See the Innocence." There was the irony again. That had been the song for which I had named that music mix. It had been right there in my ears, on my mind, and yet it took Larry and the dog to get me to stop thinking about thinking about not thinking before I could start seeing about seeing what I should be seeing.

Late that night, I called Benny's voicemail and left a message saying that I would be in the next day after all. Would he have a few minutes to see me?

In the morning he stopped by my office on his way in. He was ready to drop a new bomb on my desk.

This time I paid attention to his eyes and let the words fade to background.

I stopped and looked. Benny hadn't changed, but what I saw had. I saw the intent, but I saw more—a frightened, little kid being a bully.

Just as he started to tell me what to do, I said "Stop." He kept talking, period, but his eyes flickered slightly.

I said "Stop, Benny, stop." He stopped and his eyes were still frightened, but no longer a bully. As I changed what I was seeing, he was changing right before my eyes.

"Benny," I said, "it's not working. We're no longer partners at the work we're doing. You interfere in how I manage my team, encouraging my team to find and report on any misstep I might make. You tell me who I can socialize with. You sabotage my success by asking me to prepare for meetings that aren't happening. I can't work like this. If we can't change things, I'm going to have to quit."

"What? You can't do that. I won't allow it!" he said.

I took a deep breath and just waited, letting the silence echo his last words.

I'd know whether this relationship stood a chance by how he responded to what I said next. I decided to give the partnership I had once valued so highly one more chance.

Then, instead of reacting to what he said, instead of taking on the defensive posture that had become my usual response, I told myself, "I can do this." I called to mind all of the positives that had made our working relationship work.

He interrupted my thoughts. "You might think you're indispensable, but you're not. We'll do fine without you." Despite his words, his voice had softened showing a glimpse of humanity. It gave me hope.

Realizing I had nothing to lose, I took a deep breath relying on everything I knew about trust and truth. I simply said, "I used to love this job. I used to thrive on seeing how you and I could inspire the team to reach for more. I used to live for seeing them achieve to their highest potential. But somewhere when the team got really good, our focus shifted from seeing me succeed to pushing out the work."

Still, he tried to hold his ground. "You can't quit. You need this job," he said, but it was clear he didn't believe his own words. I could see him becoming softer as each second passed.

"When you no longer believed in me, I no longer believed in myself. I started to question everything that had made me successful in the past. I felt like I couldn't trust you anymore, but worse, I couldn't trust myself. I no longer knew when I was doing good work. The longer it happened, the weaker I became until I was ready to jump through any hoop that you placed in my path." I waited, giving my message time to sink in. Then I said, "You're wrong, Benny. I don't need a job like that."

Everything hung in the balance while we waited for what happened next.

Then finally, a Benny I'd not seen in months said, "So is that it? Shouldn't we talk about this?"

"I know I don't need this job. I have freelance opportunities and I've been thinking about writing a book," I said calmly, quietly. "Still, for the first few years, we trusted each other. The partnership we had was so strong. Back then, this was the best job I ever had. I'm still here because I couldn't walk away from that."

For the first time in months, I felt like I was myself and it was true. When I first started working with Benny we had had been exceptional. People used to remark on how well we worked together. Was there a way to start over?

We both needed some time to think about what was the best next steps.

I suggested that I take two of the ten weeks of vacation I was due and then we meet to discuss where things stood. It seemed the best chance if we wanted to re-establish the winning partnership we once knew. Either way, I wasn't worried about the outcome. Whether we found common ground or decided our partnership was dead, our answer would be the right answer.

Before I left, I told my colleagues I was taking my vacation. Then I drove home like a 65th Crayon, still feeling exuberant as I parked my car.

Just as I floated into my condo and put on my headset, Larry and the dog pulled up in an Austin-Healey Bug-Eyed Sprite. I knew now that I didn't have to tell them what happened.

We went for a celebration ride, and found ourselves on the rocks by Belmont Harbor. Larry and I drank champagne, while the dog took a swim. We planned a week's vacation somewhere warm where I could refuel. Then Larry cut to the chase.

"So did you really have a winning relationship with Benny?"

"Yeah, actually we did. I've been so busy coming to terms with the fact that Benny was treating me badly. Maybe that's why I withstood his bad behavior for so long. Maybe I just couldn't believe it was really happening. You see, for the first four years, while we were helping the team get back their confidence, I had my dream job. A company of really smart people who really cared about our customers and a boss who had the same goals and trusted me to do my best to reach them. And I trusted him. . . . "

I stopped for a few minutes to remember how good it had been. Then I went on, "until Benny melted enough to show his humanity again, I had forgotten. I had been too tied up in a need to protect myself from him. But to be fair, until Benny became afraid of my getting too much attention from the board, he had been the best boss I ever had. That's what made it all so bad. I guess I wasn't just his golden child of an employee, but he had been my golden child of boss as well."

"So," Larry said, "do you think you'll be able to get back to what you once had?"

"To be honest, I'm not at all sure. It could be that too much damage has been done to share that kind of trust again. Still,

I don't want to quit in anger. We can have a meeting in two weeks to renegotiate a new agreement. If it doesn't work then, at least we won't be throwing away good things to pay for the bad."

After some time watching the sailboats on the lake, Larry hit me with the last outstanding question.

"So, I don't suppose the world is going to take to calling you Crayon and, unlike I did for the dog, I can't really tell the world your name is 'the girl.' So why don't you pick a name you like and stick with it?" Larry suggested. Just then the dog came out of the water and shook off the lake.

I looked at the dog for a short while and said, "What do you think?" He gave me a look that said you already know. So I turned to Larry and said, "I guess I'll stick with Alice. It's worked for me so far."

I turned back to the dog and said, "And what's your name?" Those caramel eyes let me know his name, but he's not ready to share it with you.

I went running today. I still go running every day. Well, pretty much every day, except for those days when I don't really feel like it. On those days I go running twice. I don't always bring along the tree from my childhood. I find that these days, sometimes it slows me down.

Larry and the dog still show up when I run. They still like to talk about how I'm doing and what I should be doing next. And they're thrilled to be able to talk about old times, times they remember watching over me now that they can tell me they were there. Sometimes they come by just to hang out. Sometimes we take a road trip in the Packard or have adventures with other friends who live in my head.

The dog hangs around more often. I feel him sitting at my feet when I'm writing, and I like having him around. He's the perfect combination of a friend and a muse.

When Benny and I parted ways, I took on some freelance work writing, and started a blog. People who read my blog began asking, "How can I do what I want to do? How can I be the person I want to be?" I found I have a new job that I love. I spend my days teaching people, "You can do anything you put your mind to."

I don't get anxiety hangovers or worry about being judged anymore. I concentrate on seeing the innocence in everything I see. But I do still wonder whether it was Larry or the dog who had the most positive effect on me.

Acknowledgments

Acknowledgement and appreciation to the following for permission to include these previously published and copyrighted materials.

1

A HORSE WITH NO NAME
Words and Music by DEWEY BUNNELL
Copyright © 1972 (Renewed) WARNER/CHAPPELL MUSIC LTD
All Rights for the Western Hemisphere Controlled by WB MUSIC CORP.
All Rights Reserved
Used By Permission of ALFRED MUSIC

2

COOL CHANGE
Words and Music by GLENN SHORROCK
Copyright © 1979 WHEATLEY MUSIC PTY. LTD.
All rights administered by WB MUSIC CORP.
All Rights Reserved
Used By Permission of ALFRED MUSIC

3

COOL CHANGE

Words and Music by GLENN SHORROCK

Copyright © 1979 WHEATLEY MUSIC PTY. LTD.

All rights administered by WB MUSIC CORP.

All Rights Reserved

Used By Permission of ALFRED MUSIC

4

SO MUCH SKY

Words and Music by JULIA MACKLIN

Copyright © 2001 JULIA MACKLIN

All Rights Reserved

Used By Permission of ESTATE OF JULIA MACKLIN

5

WHITE SUN

Words and Music by TOM JOHNSTON

Copyright © 1972 WARNER–TAMERLANE PUBLISHING CORP.

All Rights Reserved

Used By Permission of ALFRED MUSIC

6

WHITE SUN

Words and Music by TOM JOHNSTON

Copyright © 1972 WARNER–TAMERLANE PUBLISHING CORP.

All Rights Reserved

Used By Permission of ALFRED MUSIC

About Liz Strauss

Liz is a Principal and CEO of GeniusShared, an organization dedicated to promoting achievement in the business community through understanding of how personal development fuels, defines, and limits (or amplifies) success. She is also founder of SOBCon, the game-changing business retreat that energized business growth and owner/author of the popular *Successful-Blog* (successful-blog.com).

Liz Strauss is an engaging, intelligent, and profoundly relevant author, speaker, retreat producer, and business coach. She is adept at distilling complex (and seemingly disconnected) human business ideas into elegantly simple concepts and helping leaders apply those concepts to the best steps to meet their goals. Liz speaks softly and carries a lot of street cred. The Dean of the College of Education at Bradley University described Liz by saying, "In my life, I've met five master teachers. She is one."

Liz has worked with C-Suite executives on four continents on planning strategy and accelerating business growth through better hiring, breaking down silos, team training, and coaching new managers. Liz builds communities of fiercely loyal employees and customers who bring their friends.

Liz lives in Chicago, Illinois with her husband and a world of ideas and stories inside her head. In between trips to see every country in the world, their son stops in for visits to check on the stuffed penguin on the bookcase.

About GeniusShared

Solid personal development fuels stronger business development and long term success—personally and professionally. This belief is at the core of GeniusShared, a small business led by Liz Strauss and Jane Boyd.

Working at the intersection of personal development and business development, GeniusShared offers a range of products, events and services designed especially for today's business builders.

Through it's highly connected community, GeniusShared brings together exceptional thinkers and doers who are committed to building each other's businesses while they build their own.

GeniusShared offers online courses, coaching, expert consultation and speaking engagements designed to provide a solid path toward personal development and business success for all business professionals.

GeniusShared events—retreats, workshops and gatherings— are skillfully crafted, high trust environments where participants work together to solve shared problems while simultaneously identifying action steps toward personal and business success.

Anything You Put Your Mind To has been published through GeniusShared Press, a division of GeniusShared. GeniusShared Press publications focus on topics directly related to personal development and business development.

You can sign-up to receive news, updates and more via the GeniusShared email newsletter at Successful-Blog.com, the online home of GeniusShared.

If you'd like to know more about the ideas in *Anything You Put Your Mind To*, GeniusShared products, events or services contact: Jane Boyd, Principal, GeniusShared geniusshared@gmail.com with your request.

40167767R00199

Made in the USA
San Bernardino, CA
12 October 2016